NEW PATH GETTING OVER CHINESE GRAMMAR
汉语语法新通路

Revised Version
修订版

周晓更 著
Zhou Xiaogeng

First Edition 2009

ISBN 978-7-80200-613-3
Copyright 2009 by Sinolingua
Published by Sinolingua
24 Baiwanzhuang Road, Beijing 100037, China
Tel: (86)10-68320585
Fax: (86)10-68326333
http://www.sinolingua.com.cn
E-mail: hyjx@sinolingua.com.cn
Printed by Beijing Foreign Languages Printing House
Distributed by China International Book Trading Corporation
35 Chegongzhuang Xilu, P.O. Box 399
Beijing 100044, China

Printed in the People's Republic of China

Contents

Chapter 1   **About the Chinese Characters**   1

Chapter 2   **Creating New Words**   9

Chapter 3   **Basic Rules for Combining Words**   21
     Section 1: Where Both Words Refer to Objects   22
     Section 2: Where Words Refer to Objects and States   28
     Section 3: Where Both Words Refer to States   32
     Section 4: Where Both Words Refer to Actions   36
     Section 5: Where Words Refer to Objects and Actions   41
     Section 6: Where Words Refer to States and Actions   50
     Section 7: Summary   54

Chapter 4   **Advanced Skills in Application**   63
     Section 1: The Construction of Complex Words   63
     Section 2: Principles and Practical Skills   71

Chapter 5   **Sentence Construction**   82
     Section 1: Typical structure: Orders and Suggestions   84
     Section 2: Typical Structure: Describing the Actions   92
     Section 3: Typical Structure: Describing the Subject   99
     Section 4: Typical Structure: Describing Existence   106
     Section 5: Special Structures   114

Chapter 6   **Specifying Tenses**   127

Chapter 7   **Raising a Question**   140
     Section 1: Questions Requiring Confirmation   142
     Section 2: Questioning Specific Components   148

Chapter 8   **Constructing Complex Sentences**   156

Chapter 9   **Advanced Skills in Making Sentences**   169

Chapter 1
About the Chinese Characters

As one of the most ancient of languages, the Chinese language remains vigorous; it is spoken by the largest population in the world and attracts increasing attention from people outside the mysterious Eastern land of its origin. Let us begin by looking into the Chinese characters, the visual messengers of this ancient language.

About 5,000 years ago, the earliest Chinese characters appeared as simple strokes carved on animal bones. These carvings are the original forms of the modern characters in use today. The ancient Chinese authors of these extraordinary characters also created the highly practical and flexible grammar system. Chinese philosophy and aesthetics have contributed to a vast, unique and marvelous culture and the ancient characters are symbols of that wisdom.

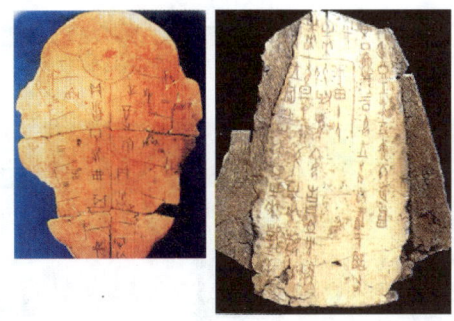

One important method in creating new characters is to imitate objects with simple strokes, like making naturalistic drawings. These original pictographic characters underwent a long evolution that led to their eventual simplification into the modern characters we see today. The following examples show how this happened.

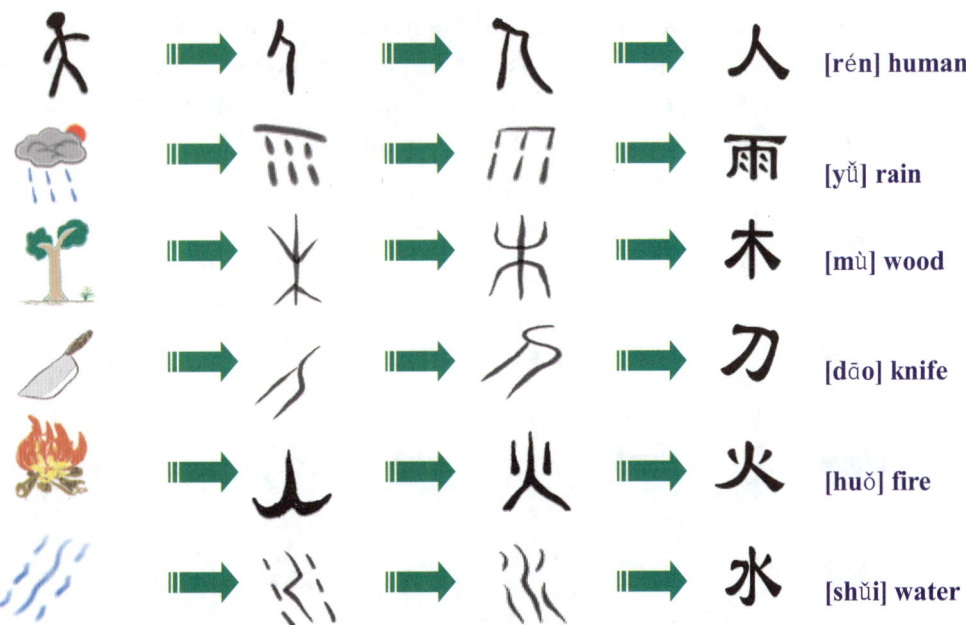

Chapter 1 About the Chinese Characters

Note: there are only a few original characters left today, and one can scarcely find any trace of the original pictographs in their present appearance.

Based on the above pictographic characters, people developed a method of creating new characters. By adding more strokes to an existing character, people created a new character referring to the specific part of a subject. In most cases, the new character has a different pronunciation from the original one. The following examples show the basic mechanism:

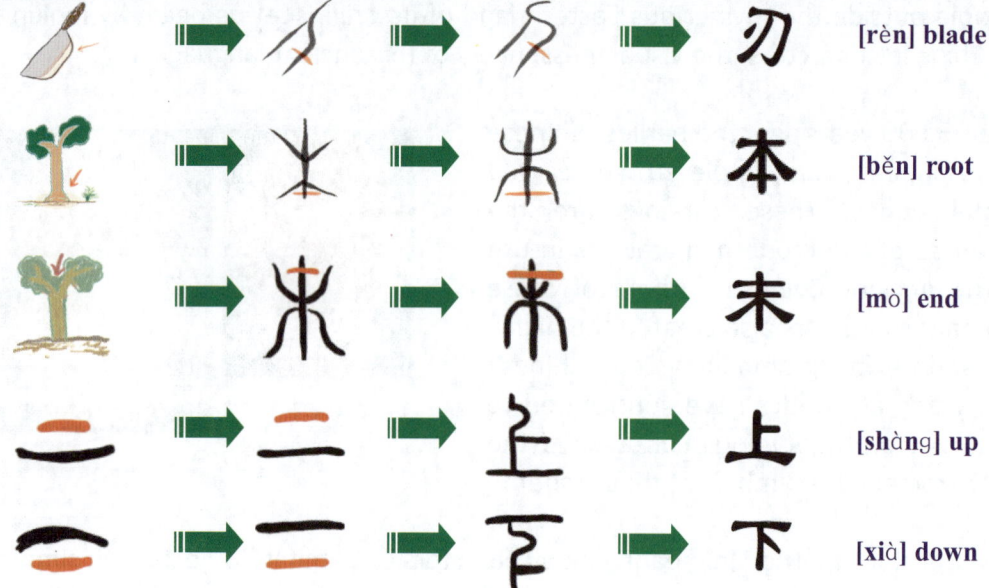

Another method of creating a new character for a new subject or concept is to integrate two or more existing characters. As every original character in the newly created character retain their own meaning, the meaning of the new character usually comes from a natural deduction of the combined original meanings. That is to say, in most cases, we can deduce the meaning of these kinds of "created" characters from their internal structures. The following examples show this mechanism:

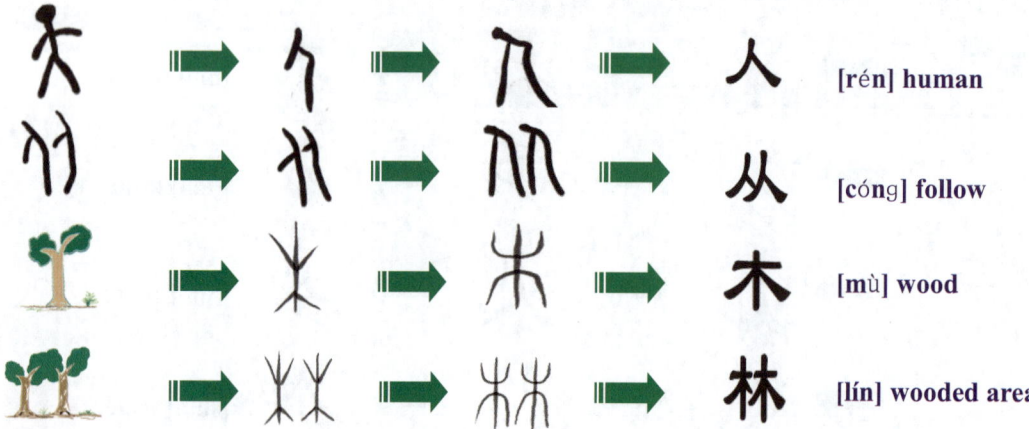

Chapter 1 About the Chinese Characters

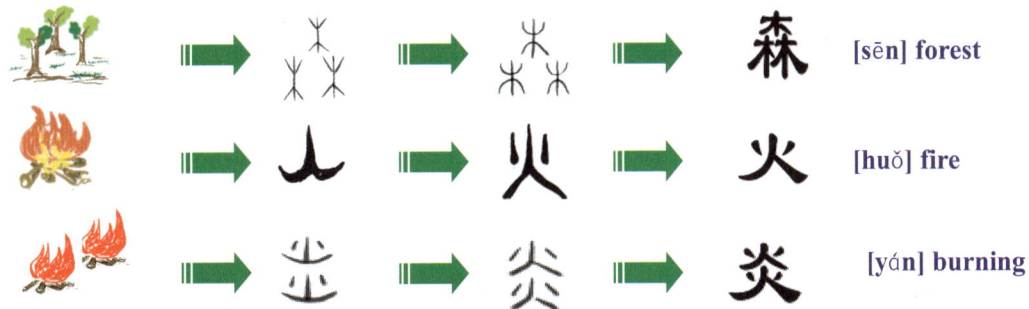

[sēn] forest

[huǒ] fire

[yán] burning

With the expansion of civilization, people had to cope with rapidly expanding social lives that required a larger number of characters for the objects and ideas that continually emerged. The above three methods of creating new characters based on the pictographic characters however, are not capable of such dynamism. Many objects (both physical objects as well as abstract concepts) are too complex for pictographs. Thus, a more complicated method of creating characters developed, one that progressed through two steps.

Step 1: Select one existing character to indicate the pronunciation, and then integrate it with another existing character (or two, or even more) to create a new character.

Step 2: Stipulate the meaning of the newly made character.

The following chart shows the basic mechanism involved.

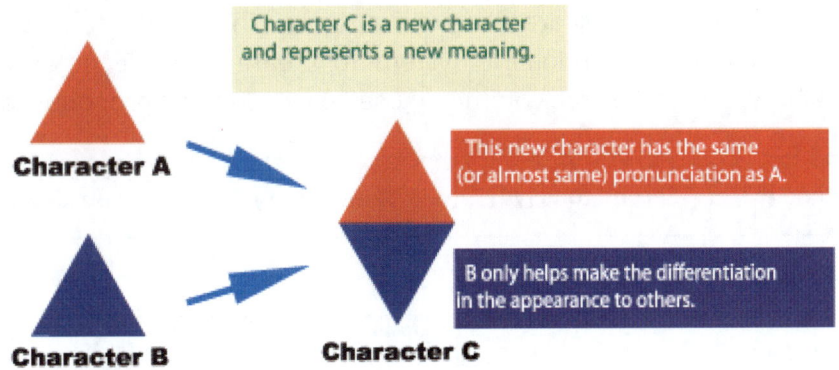

When A and B are integrated together to be a new character, they can be flexibly structured into a whole.

Examples:

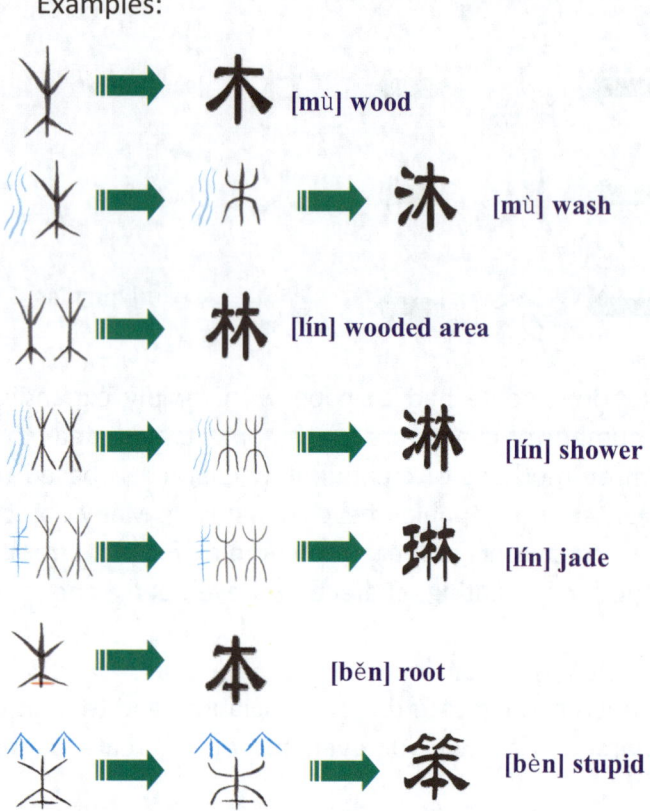

The advantage of this method is that people can integrate existing characters to create new characters, which provides extensive possibilities for creating new descriptions and meanings. What's more, the characters integrated into the new characters usually offer strong clues to their pronunciation. The disadvantage is that many characters frequently share one pronunciation. Therefore, the Chinese language adopted four tones in its phonetic system to create a subtle differentiation. For example, below is a list of some commonly used characters, all pronounced as [yu]:

First tone [yū]		**Second tone [yú]**		**Third tone [yǔ]**		**Fourth tone [yù]**	
迂	winding	与	with, to	与	against, with	与	to participate
纡	tortuous	鱼	fish	屿	island	玉	jade
淤	silt	于	at, to, on	予	to give, to grant	驭	to ride, to lead
瘀	stasis	盂	jar, pot	伛	hunchback	芋	taro
於	a surname	予	me	宇	eaves, space	吁	to appeal

		余	spare, surplus	羽	feather	峪	valley, ravine
		臾	moment	雨	rain	浴	bath; to bathe
		腴	plump	俣	big, large	欲	desire, need
		渔	fishery	语	language, words	裕	abundant
		隅	corner, nook	圄	horse stable	郁	lush, gloomy
		愚	stupid			育	to raise
		俞	a surname			狱	jail, prison
		揄	to draw			域	scope, boundary
		逾	to exceed			预	in advance
		渝	to alter			谕	to instruct
		愉	pleased			喻	metaphor
		瑜	jade			愈	more; to heal
		榆	elm			遇	to meet
		娱	to amuse			寓	to reside;
		虞	to predict			御	to ride, to control
		舆	carriage			誉	reputation, fame

    This has proved to be the easiest and most efficient method of creating characters in history. More than 90% of Chinese characters currently in use were created in this fashion.

    In the evolution of the language, the Chinese ancestors seemed to be very diligent in creating new characters, so diligent in fact, that at one time there were more than 40,000 characters. This proved problematic for the practical use of the language because most people could hardly recognize the vast number of characters involved.

Chapter 1 About the Chinese Characters

People love simple and easy things, and this preference inevitably led to simplifying the entire language system. During the past 5,000 years, people have been developing this ancient language into a powerful and efficient tool. Along the way, many outmoded characters vanished while many new characters evolved, and people became more proficient in the language. There have been several significant breakthroughs in the past 100 years. Obvious improvements include:

1. The colloquial language system dominated the daily language.

2. Some Western manners of writing and reading were popularly adopted.

3. Many traditional characters were restructured and simplified with fewer strokes.

Mandarin has now become the standard language of the Chinese nation, reduced in size to the roughly 2,600 characters most commonly used in people's daily language. A key factor that makes it possible to reduce the amount of characters used daily to a reasonable level lies in the construction of the vocabulary system. As we will discuss in the next chapter, the Chinese adopted a unique approach for that, along with more effective and efficient methods.

Chapter 1 About the Chinese Characters

 Extra Knowledge: Origins of Chinese Characters

Most ancient Chinese characters changed tremendously in both appearance and pronunciation during their evolution. Today, it is very hard to find the traces of their original appearance. In the course of creating new characters, some characters or strokes are found frequently integrated with others, and they are regarded as the earliest traceable form, or etyma, from which new words are derived. These etyma usually provide strong hints to the meanings of the characters. For example, when a character contains 目 in its structure, it usually refers to something related to eyes.

 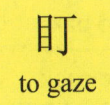   

Another example: characters with 口 usually refer to something related with the mouth.

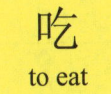 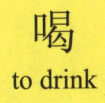 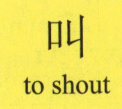 

吐 to split

Below is a list of the most popularly used etyma that provide strong hints to meanings. (There are, of course, many exceptions and this is only a general view.)

Etyma	Related meaning	Examples
刂	to cut, to divide	割 to cut　刮 to scratch　刻 to carve
人亻	people, human	仙 fairy　体 body　你 you
冫	cold, ice	冷 cold　凉 cool　冻 frost
口	mouth	叼 to hold in mouth　叹 to sigh
土	land, earth, soil	地 land　坛 altar　坝 dam
女	female, feminine	妻 wife　妇 married woman　她 she
宀	house, shelter	家 home　宅 house　室 room
山	mountain, land, soil	岸 shore　岩 rock　崖 cliff
巾	clothing, dress	帽 cap, hat　布 cloth　帐 curtain

Chapter 1 About the Chinese Characters

亻	to walk, to move, to labor	行 to walk 征 to levy 徙 to migrate
忄	feeling, emotion; to think	记 to memorize 忆 to remember
扌	act, behavior, movement	打 to hit, to beat 拉 to pull 推 to push
日	sun, light, time, season	春 spring 旺 prosperous 映 to reflect
木	wood; wooden	桌 table 椅 chair 板 board
氵	water, river	海 sea 江 river 溪 brook
火	fire	烟 smoke 烤 to bake 炉 oven
灬	fire; to cook	煮 to boil 烹 to cook 煎 to fry
犭	animal, beast	猎 to hunt 狗 dog 猫 cat
疒	sick, disease	病 sick 疾 disease 疗 to cure, to treat
目	eye, view, sight	眼 eye 盲 blind 看 to watch
石	stone	矿 mineral resource 砂 sand 硬 hard
米	food, cereal	粮 cereal 籽 seed 粥 congee
纟	silk, cloth; to weave	丝 silk 织 to weave 纺 to weave
舟	boat, vessel	船 boat 舰 vessel 艇 boat
艹	plant, wood	草 grass 芽 bud 花 flower
虫	reptile, insect	蛇 snake 虾 shrimp 蛙 frog
讠	words, language	说 to say 谈 to talk 论 to comment
辶	to walk, to move; journey	巡 to patrol 远 far 追 to chase
酉	wine, alcohol	酒 wine 醉 drunk 酿 to brew
钅	metal	钉 nail 铁 iron 铜 cooper
雨	rain, water, weather	雷 thunder 雾 fog 霜 frost
饣	food, meal	饭 meal, food 饿 hungry 饮 to drink
鸟	birds	鸡 cock, hen 鹅 goose 鹦鹉 parrot
竹	bamboo, plant	笛 flute 竿 pole 筛 sieve
足	foot; to walk	跳 to jump 蹦 to leap 跃 to spring

Chapter 2
Creating New Words

The essential goal in creating new characters is to create symbols for the subjects (a physical item, an abstract concept, etc.). The correspondence between a symbol (character) and the subject can be defined as the "meaning" of the symbol. Almost every character has its own meaning and can be defined as a "word". The independent characters build up the basic vocabulary of the Chinese language.

It also frequently happens that one character has more than two or more meanings. Sometimes these meanings relate to each other, at other times they have nothing in common. This phenomenon is the result of the continuing evolution of the Chinese language. Thus, in most cases, a character should be regarded as a random collection of the meanings, whether they are related to each other or not. The following examples show the diversity of meanings of Chinese characters.

发(fā):
1. to send out; to issue, to deliver, to distribute. Examples: 发射, 发送
2. to utter, to express. Examples: 发言, 发音
3. to discharge, to shoot, to emit. Examples: 发光, 发热
4. to develop, to expand. Examples: 发展, 发扬
5. (of foodstuffs) to ferment. Examples: 发酵, 发霉
6. to generate; to bring into existence. Examples: 发电, 发病
7. to open up; to discover, to explore. Examples: 发现, 揭发
8. to get into a certain state; to become. Examples: 发痒, 发苦
9. to show one's feeling. Examples: 发怒, 发笑
10. to start; to set out. Examples: 发车, 发船
11. as a quantifier. Examples: 一发子弹, 一发炮弹

Sometimes, a character has various pronunciations with various meanings. For example:

和 (hé):
1. gentle, mild, kind. Examples: 温和, 缓和
2. harmonious. Examples: 和睦, 和谐
3. peace. Examples: 和平, 媾和
4. (sports) to draw, to tie. Examples: 和棋, 和局
5. together with
6. and
7. sum. Example: 总和
8. a surname

Chapter 2 Creating New Words

和 (hè)
1. to join in (singing). Example: 附和
2. to compose a poem in reply. Examples: 和词，和曲

和 (huó)
1. to mix (powder) with water. Examples: 和面，和泥

和 (hú)
1. to win (especially in the Chinese game of mah-jongg)

Theoretically speaking, we can create new characters for any subject that might emerge, but that is not necessarily feasible because it would produce too many characters. Therefore, we face a dilemma: on the one hand, we need to keep the number of characters at a reasonable level; on the other hand, there must be some way to create "names" for the items and concepts constantly emerging from our fast-paced civilization. The Chinese language adopts a unique approach in resolving this problem.

Every subject has its features or properties, and it is possible to differentiate each subject by its most essential features and properties. Therefore, the existing characters that best capture the features and properties of the new subject can be used to describe a subject. The exterior appearance of the new character comes from two (or more) characters that are combined and integrated, functioning as a new word for that subject. The following chart shows the mechanism involved:

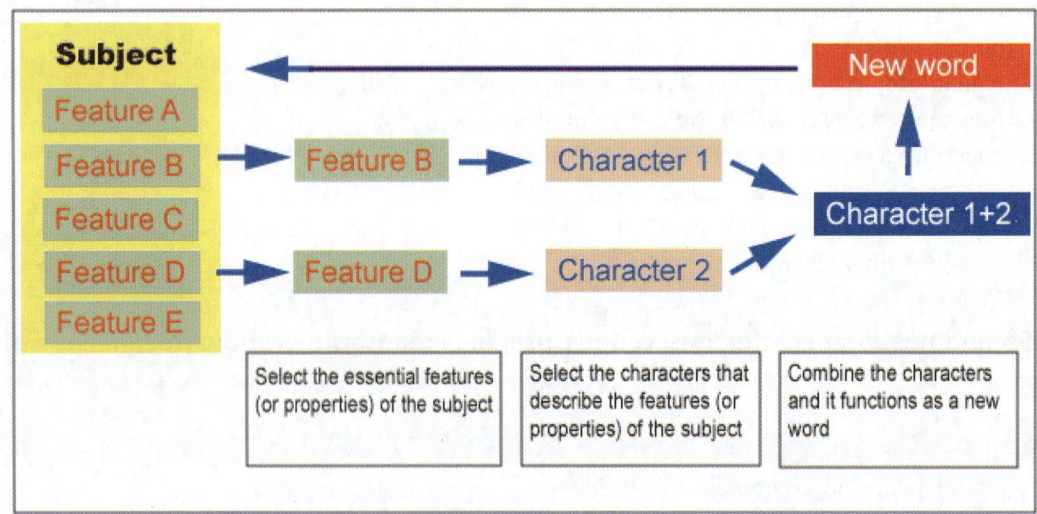

The following two examples on words for horses show how this process works.

The description of a horse can include two categories, one is "mare", and the other is "stone horse". Two characters were created for the two categories:

Chapter 2 Creating New Words

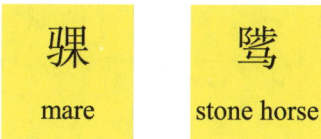

These two categories can be regarded as subjects with different features. For the mare, these essential features include:

1. It belongs to the horse species.
2. Its gender is female.

For the "stone-horse", these essential features include:

1. It belongs to the horse species.
2. Its gender is male.

At the same time, there are characters specifically created for these features:

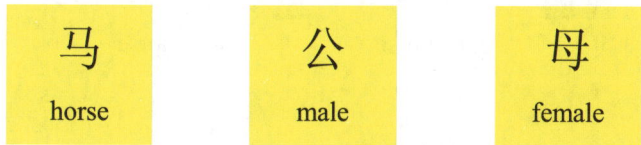

As shown below, the above characters can be combined to make new words for these subjects.

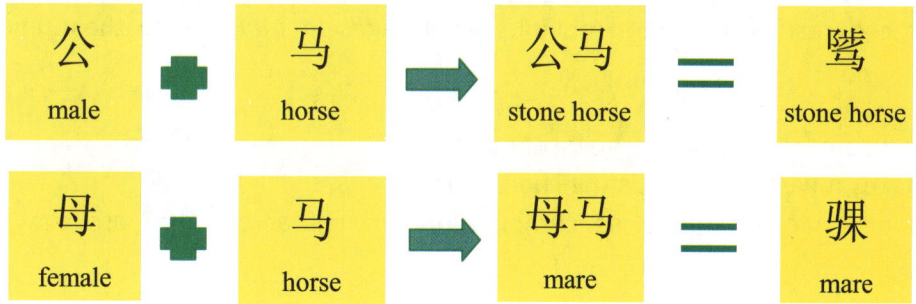

The following characters were created for horses of various colors.

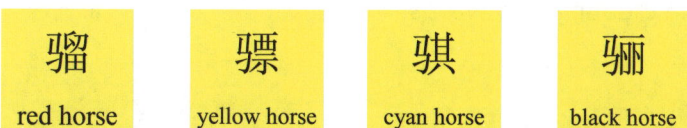

Chapter 2 Creating New Words

The following characters are for the colors:

We can combine the four different subjects in the following way:

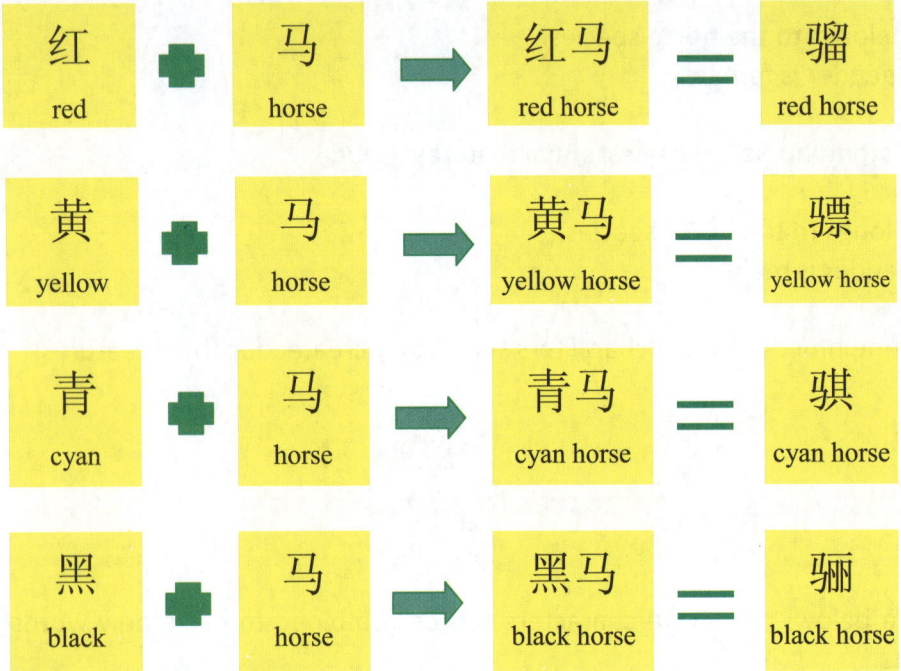

This method results in several obvious advantages in building up the Chinese vocabulary:

1. There is no need to create new characters.
2. It makes full use of the existing characters.
3. The new words appear as combinations of characters that are easy to understand.

The above examples only show the essence of the mechanism used to create new words by the interaction of meanings. The following examples show the effectiveness and efficiency of this method in creating new words.

Chapter 2 Creating New Words

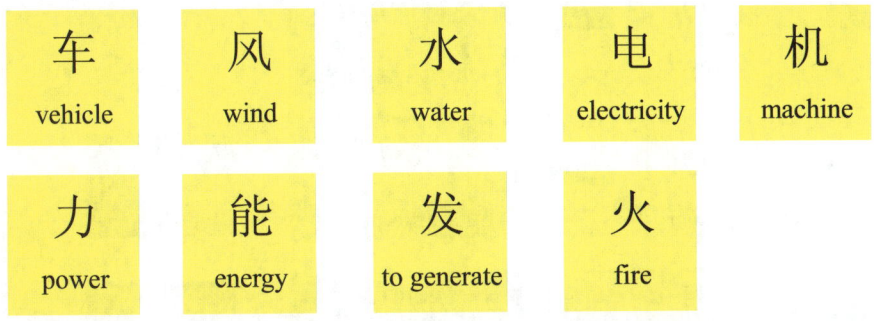

车 vehicle	风 wind	水 water	电 electricity	机 machine
力 power	能 energy	发 to generate	火 fire	

Below are all the words that are created by combining the above characters:

水 water	＋ 车 vehicle	→	水车 mill wheel 
风 wind	＋ 车 vehicle	→	风车 windmill 
电 electricity	＋ 车 vehicle	→	电车 trolley 
火 fire	＋ 车 vehicle	→	火车 train 
风 wind	＋ 能 energy	→	风能 wind energy 
电 electricity	＋ 能 energy	→	电能 electric energy 
水 water	＋ 能 energy	→	水能 hydraulic energy 
风 wind	＋ 力 power	→	风力 wind power 

Chapter 2 Creating New Words

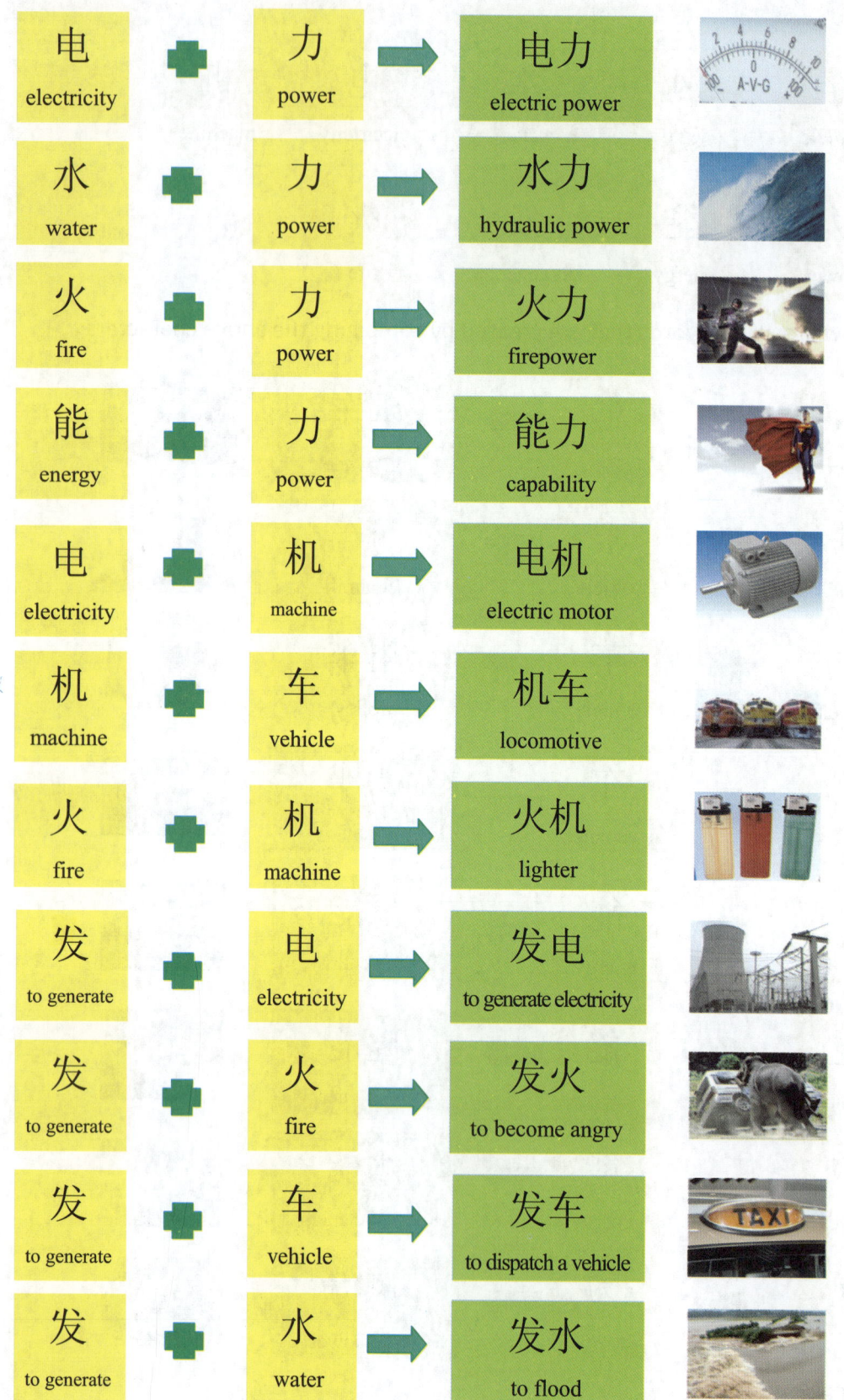

Chapter 2 Creating New Words

This mechanism, along with the principles and rules, govern the Chinese grammar system's creation of words, phrases and even entire sentences. Based on the above words, we can create new words and phrases by repeatedly applying these basic principles and rules.

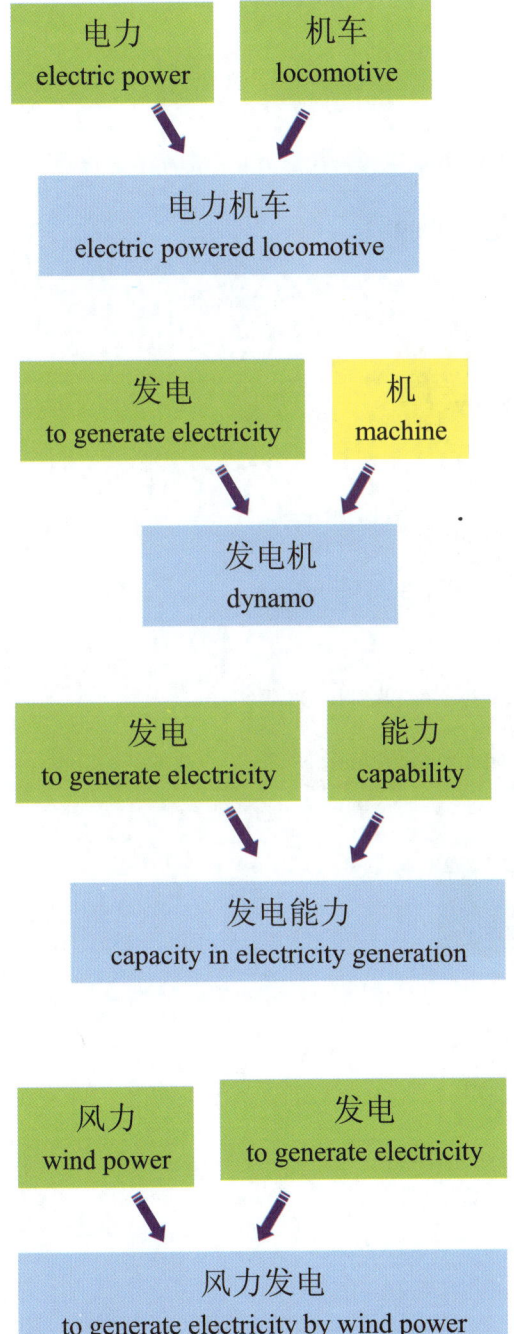

Chapter 2 Creating New Words

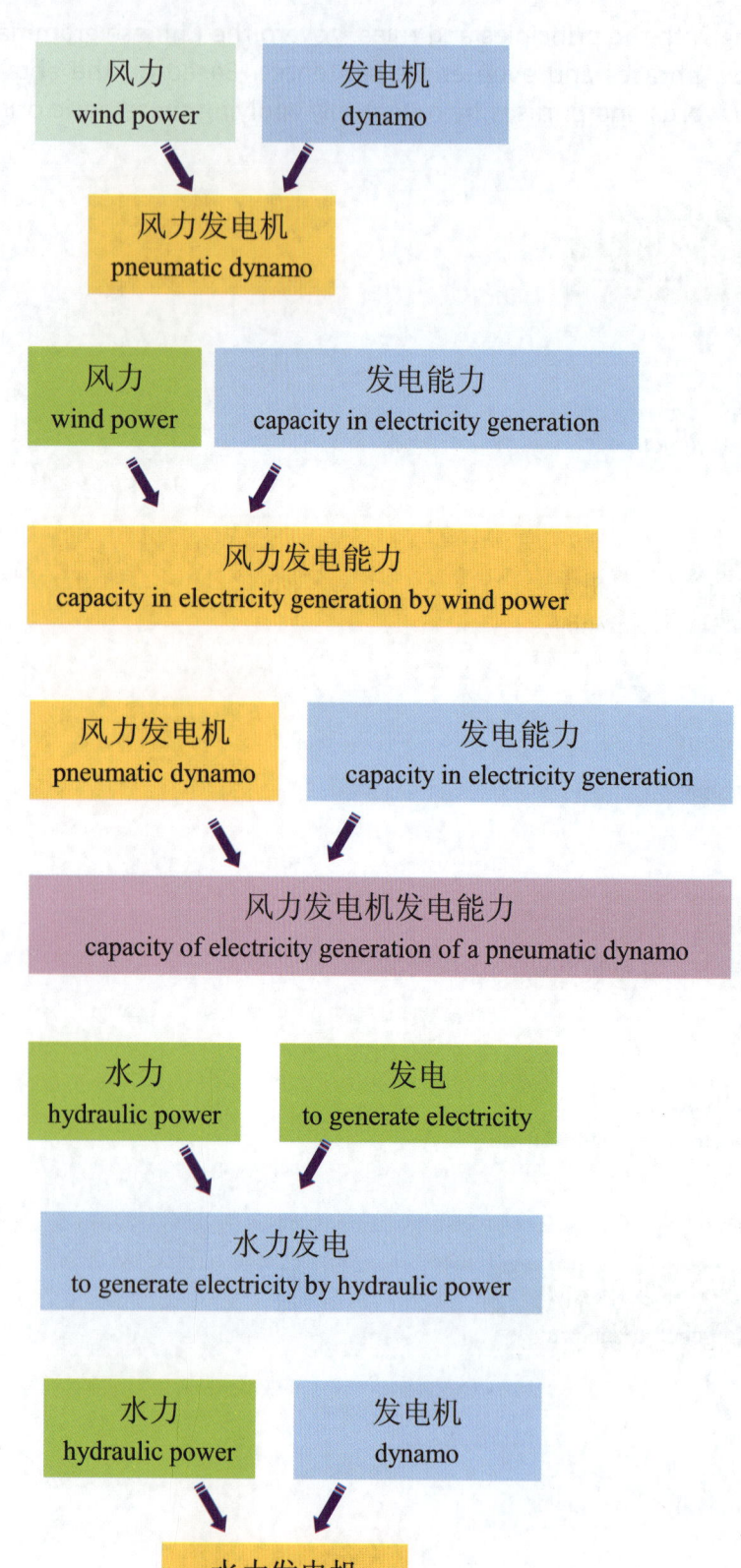

Chapter 2 Creating New Words

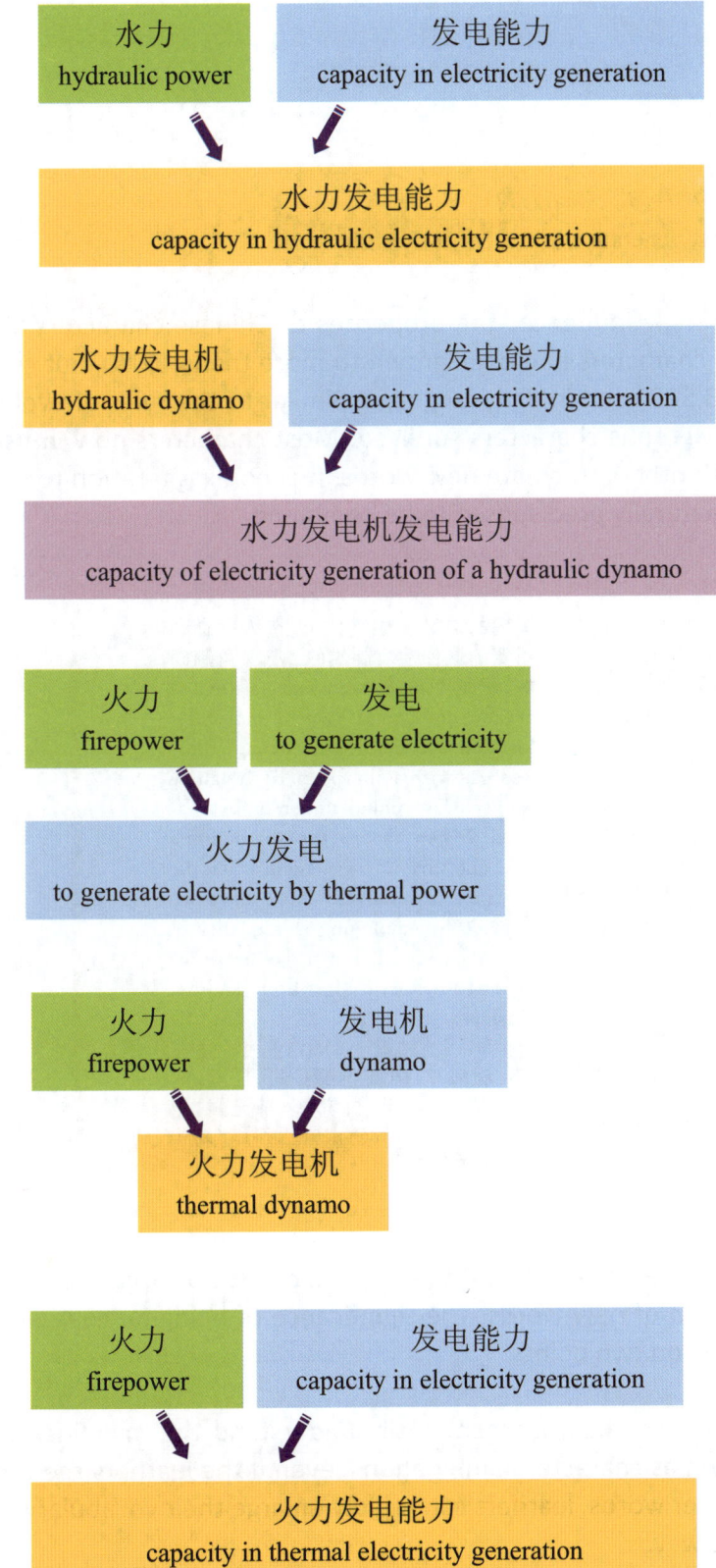

Chapter 2 Creating New Words

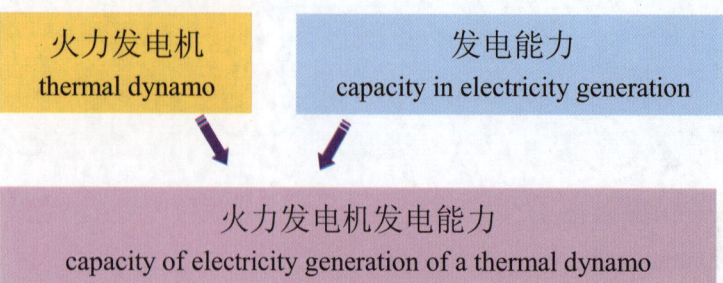

This mechanism also strongly influences the properties of Chinese characters. As noted above, the number of characters had once grown to more than 40,000, but currently there are only about 3,500 used in daily language. Similar to the rules of evolution, only the essential and vigorous characters survived. Most characters now in use can be flexibly combined with others to create new words. It is no exaggeration to say that Chinese characters are naturally predisposed to be combined.

Based on the mechanisms described above, there formed a set of principles and rules used to guide the creation of new words. The significance of being familiar with these principles and rules rests on two points:

1. The principles and the rules help learners easily understand the meanings of such words (or phrases) shown as character combinations, even if the learners see the words for the first time. In other words, learners can rapidly enlarge their vocabulary in a more efficient and effective way.

Chapter 2 Creating New Words

2. The principles and rules are powerful and practical tools for learners in their actual application. They can "create" words freely and reasonably according to their needs by using these principles and rules. The precondition is that they should be familiar with the characters.

♛ Extra Knowledge: Evolution of the Chinese Language

In ancient Chinese books, characters are in their traditional forms and typeset vertically without punctuation. This format makes it difficult to read and comprehend the text. Currently, these traditional characters are rarely used in Chinese mainland.

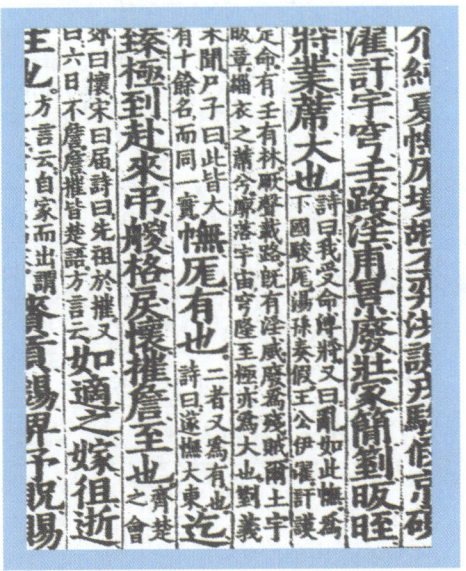

Mandarin is now the official language of China and is widely promoted. In fact, there was no such language in Chinese history. Mandarin is an artificial language based on the Beijing accent and North China's vocabulary and grammar system. It has been a difficult long-term project to popularize Mandarin throughout China because many dialects still dominate daily language in a number of areas. There is no doubt that this popularization of Mandarin will bring a necessary efficiency to people's communication throughout the country.

There are a set of rules guiding the sequence of strokes in writing a character. Good habits in writing help make a nice calligraphy. Examples:

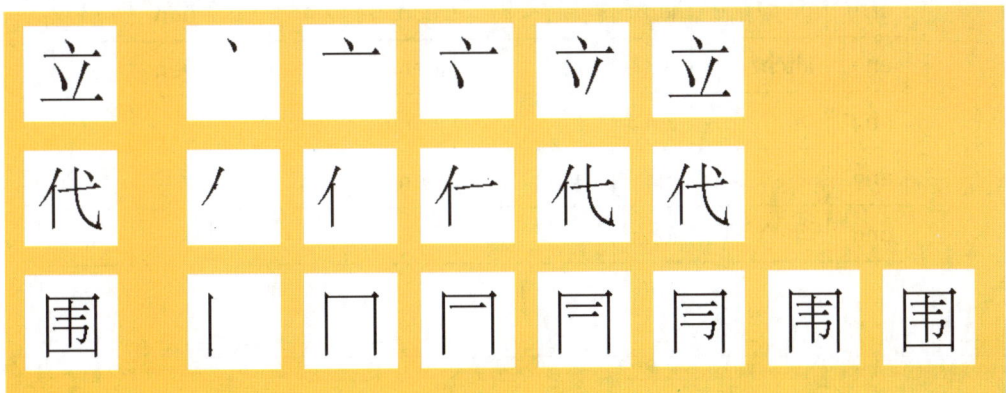

019

Chapter 2 Creating New Words

 Quick Reference: Chinese Spelling System

Below is a list of all the initial consonants and vowels, along with their approximate pronunciations:

Initial Consonants

b	boar	p	polar	m	more	f	before
d	decided	t	deter	n	nurse	l	learn
g	girl	k	handkerchief	h	her	j	jitter
q	cheetah	x	she	zh	giraffe	ch	catch
sh	bush	r	interest	z	hands	c	cats
s	sir						

Vowels

		i	if	u	look	ü	---
a	ah	ia	Columbia	ua	---		
o	or			uo	tour		
e	flower	ie	year			üe	---
ai	I			uai	why		
ei	lake			uei	way		
ao	cow	iao	---				
ou	slow	iou	u				
an	plan	ian		uan	one	üan	---
en	kitchen	in	In	uen	when	üen	---
ang	on	iang		uang	want		
eng	---	ing	trying	ueng	---		
ong	don't	iong					

Chapter 3
Basic Rules for Combining Words

The meanings of characters can be placed into three main categories:

1. Characters referring to concrete objects, such as a door, a window, a car, a dog, a flower,

2. Characters referring to actions, such as eat, drink, walk, and run,

3. Characters referring to an abstract state, such as yellow, red, cold, hot, fast, slow, high, low, etc.

There are six main types of meanings used when combining characters:

1. Two characters both in category 1;

2. Two characters both in category 2;

3. Two characters both in category 3;

4. One character in category 1 and one in 2;

5. One character in category 1 and one in 3;

6. One character in category 2 and one in 3.

In the following sections, we will go into detail about each of these types. In order to simplify the presentation, we will discuss the principles and rules in the various combinations of only two characters.

Chapter 3 Basic Rules for Combining Words

Section 1: Where Both Words Refer to Objects

There are three basic cases for combining characters referring to concrete objects.

Case 1:

Sometimes, two characters have the same meaning, or almost the same meaning. They can be combined to get a new word that refers to the same (or very similar) meaning as the characters. For example:

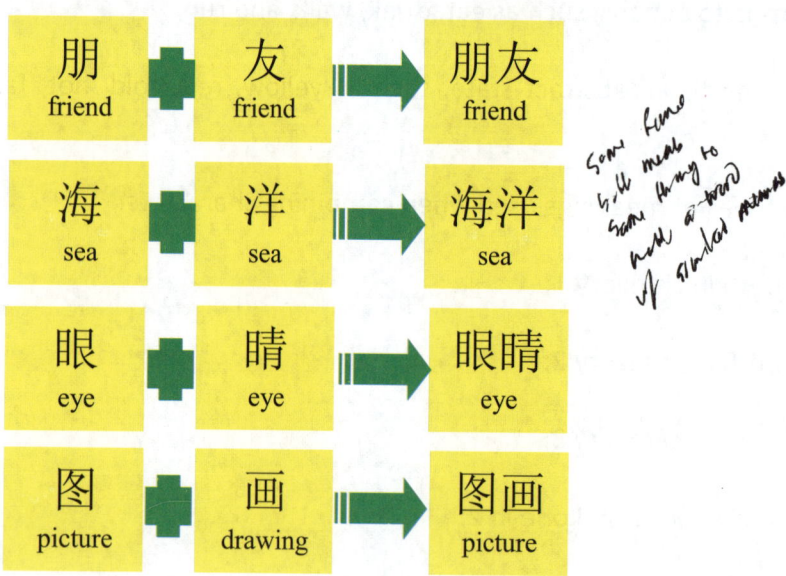

Such words lessen the possibility of misunderstanding caused by the homophones without changing the original meaning. It is quite common that tens of characters share one pronunciation, which easily causes confusion in spoken language. By this method, we can get a word with a complex pronunciation that markedly reduces the influence of homophones without changing the original meaning. Other examples:

法 law + 律 regulation　----　法律 law, regulation
群 crowd + 众 crowd　----　群众 crowd
道 reason + 理 reason　----　道理 reason
道 road + 路 road　----　道路 road
价 price + 值 value　----　价值 price, value
门 door + 户 door　----　门户 door
机 machine + 器 apparatus　----　机器 machine, apparatus
声 sound + 音 sound　----　声音 sound

Sometimes, such combinations also refer to a whole category. For example:

Here, in addition to the meaning houses, 房屋 also means all kinds of house-type buildings. Other examples:

土 soil + 地 land ---- 土地 land
天 sky + 空 air ---- 天空 air, universe
江 river + 河 river ---- 江河 all rivers
人 people + 民 public ---- 人民 people
图 picture + 像 figure ---- 图像 image, figures
身 body + 体 body ---- 身体 body of a creature
庭 yard + 院 court ---- 庭院 garden, yard

Case 2:

The combination of two characters that refer to opposite meanings usually produces a word that refers to a whole category. For example:

Here, 春 and 秋 are two opposite seasons in a year, and the combination refers to the full category of seasons - a whole year. Other examples:

天 sky + 地 earth ---- 天地 space, universe
饭 staple food + 菜 dish ---- 饭菜 meal, food
姓 surname + 名 family name ---- 姓名 name
岁 year + 月 month ---- 岁月 time
水 water + 土 soil ---- 水土 natural environment
事 affair + 物 object ---- 事物 things

Case 3:

In Chapter 2, we introduced the basic mechanism for creating new words by combining the characters referring to the essential features of a subject. Although the meanings of the characters are independent of each other, the characters can still be combined to describe the essential features of a subject, thus the combination functions as a new word.

Chapter 3 Basic Rules for Combining Words

This is a very productive method of creating new words, and there are numerous such words in the vocabulary. The principle in constructing such words is that the character referring to the most essential feature of the subject is always placed at the end of the combination. For example:

Note: Most of these words above are already fixed, leaving almost no margin to create new ones.

In the Chinese language, some characters can function as prefixes or suffixes. When combined with other characters, they have no influence on the meaning but bring an easiness and fluency to the pronunciation. The most commonly used are 头, 子, and 儿. For example:

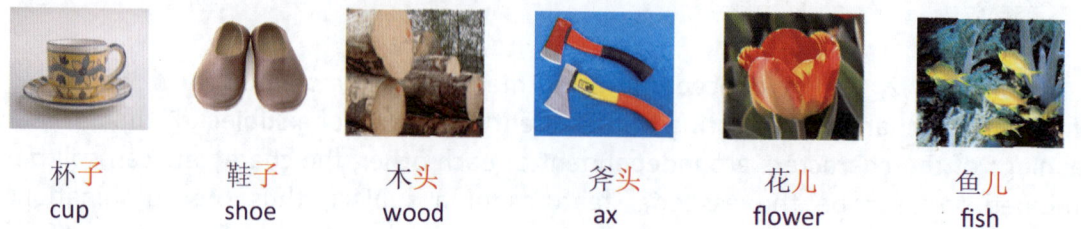

Chapter 3 Basic Rules for Combining Words

 Key Application: Quantity-Quantifier Structure

1. In Chinese, there are words that correspond to words used in English to identify or refer to people or things.

English	Chinese
I, me	我
we, us	我们
you (single)	你
you (plural)	你们
he, him	他
they (male)	他们
she, her	她
they (female)	她们
it	它
they (non human beings)	它们

this	这
these	这些 *
that	那
those	那些 *

zhè xiē

* 这些 and 那些: 些 can be substituted by other quantifiers according to specific situations.

2. In Chinese there is no plural form for words, when we want to specify the plural of an object we usually add 们 after the word. Examples:

你 you + 们 ---- 你们 you (plural)
他 he + 们 ---- 他们 they
朋友 friend + 们 ---- 朋友们 friends   *péng you men* 朋友们
男人 man + 们 ---- 男人们 men
孩子 child + 们 ---- 孩子们 children
猴子 monkey + 们 ---- 猴子们 monkeys

In addition to the above, we can also use a quantity-quantifier structure, which will be discussed below.

In the Chinese language, we usually use a quantity-quantifier structure when we mention a certain subject (people, animal, things, matters, concepts, etc.). The basic structure is as follows:

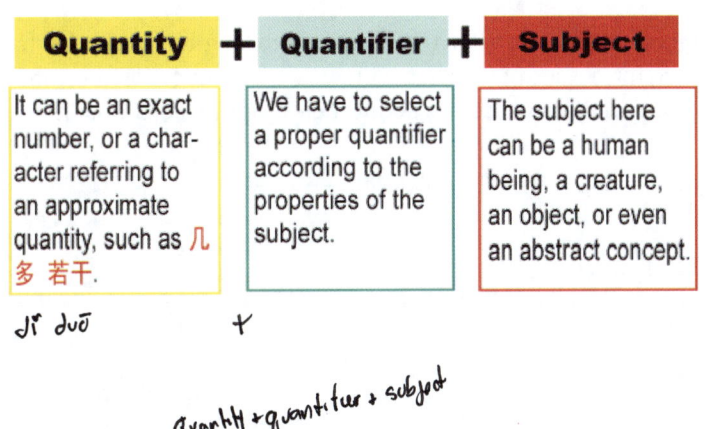

Quantity + **Quantifier** + **Subject**

Quantity	Quantifier	Subject
It can be an exact number, or a character referring to an approximate quantity, such as 几 多 若干.	We have to select a proper quantifier according to the properties of the subject.	The subject here can be a human being, a creature, an object, or even an abstract concept.

jǐ duō

quantity + quantifier + subject

Chapter 3 Basic Rules for Combining Words

Examples:

三 three + 个 quantifier for people + 朋友 friend ---- 三个朋友 three friends
一千 one thousand + 名 quantifier for people + 学生 student ---- 一千名学生 one thousand students
数百 several hundreds + 本 quantifier for books + 书 book ---- 数百本书 several hundreds of books
几十 tens of + 封 quantifier for item sealed + 信 letter ---- 几十封信 tens of letters

The key point in using such a structure is to select a proper quantifier for the specific subject (human or non-human). Generally speaking, there are several main categories of quantifiers:

1. Scientific Quantifiers

These are the units for scientific measurements, such as 公斤 (kilograms), 公里 (kilometer), etc. For example:

三 three + 公斤 kilogram + 苹果 apple ---- 三公斤苹果 three kilograms of apples
一 one + 公里 kilometer + 距离 distance ---- 一百公里距离 a distance of one hundred kilometers
八 eight + 克 gram + 黄金 gold ---- 八克黄金 eight grams of gold

Quick Reference: Commonly Used Quantifiers for Chinese Measurements

weight: 斤 half kilograms   两 tale (50 grams)   担 50 kilograms
length: 里 500 meters   丈 3.33 meters   尺 1/3 meter
          寸 1/3 decimeter
area: 亩 about 666 square meters   分 about 66.6 square meters
volume: 斗 1 deciliter

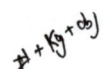

2．Chinese traditional quantifiers

Chinese traditional quantifiers have arisen through long-term use. You have to select a proper quantifier for a specific subject. Below is a collection of the most commonly used quantifiers, you can find the details about their usage in a dictionary.

个 位 名 头 台 朵 场 面 件 本 张 片 只 行 页 尊 扇
架 枝 艘 句 段 篇 间 把 条 根 匹 块 辆 幅 座 章 首

Examples:

六 six + 匹 + 马 horse ---- 六匹马 six horses
四 four + 只 (or 头) + 羊 sheep ---- 四只（头）羊 four sheep

026

Chapter 3 Basic Rules for Combining Words

两 two + 盏 + 灯 lamp ---- 两盏灯 two lamps
几 several + 位 + 客人 guest ---- 几位客人 several guests
好多 many + 辆 + 汽车 vehicle ---- 好多辆车 many vehicles

3. External quantifiers

They are frequently used to indicate the existing state of the object. In theory, any format of container or package can be used as a quantifier. What you need to do is to find the proper word. For example:

五 five + 瓶 bottle + 水 water ---- 五瓶水 five bottles of water
七 seven + 箱 case + 衣服 clothes ---- 五箱衣服 five cases of clothing
几十 tens of + 袋 bag + 大米 rice ---- 几十袋大米 tens of bags of rice
六 six + 集装箱 container + 货 goods ---- 六集装箱货 six containers of goods

4. Quantifiers for groups. There are strict requirements in selecting quantifiers in accordance with various subjects, just as there are in traditional quantifiers. The most commonly used are:

堆 pile   对 pair   双 pair   副 pair   套 suit   队 line   伙 group   批 batch
群 group 帮 group 班 group 串 line   拨 group 列 row   行 column 排 line
系列 series   捆 bunch 摞 pile   打 dozen

Examples:

一 one + 群 group + 学生 student ---- 一群学生 (a group of students)
一 one + 系列 series + 问题 problem ---- 一系列问题 a series of problems
几 several + 批 batch + 产品 product ---- 几批产品 several batches of products
几 several + 堆 pile + 沙子 sands ---- 几堆沙子 several piles of sands

We can also use the quantity-quantifier structure for actions, which we will discuss later.

Chapter 3 Basic Rules for Combining Words

Section 2: Where Words Refer to Objects and States

A character referring to an abstract state (冷 cold, 热 hot, 高 high, 低 low, 大 big, 小 small, etc.) can be combined with a character referring to an object to make a word with a more specific meaning. There are three basic cases in this kind of combination:

Case 1:

This follows the typical mechanism of creating new words: both characters describe the essential features of a subject, and the combination of them equals a word for that object. Example:

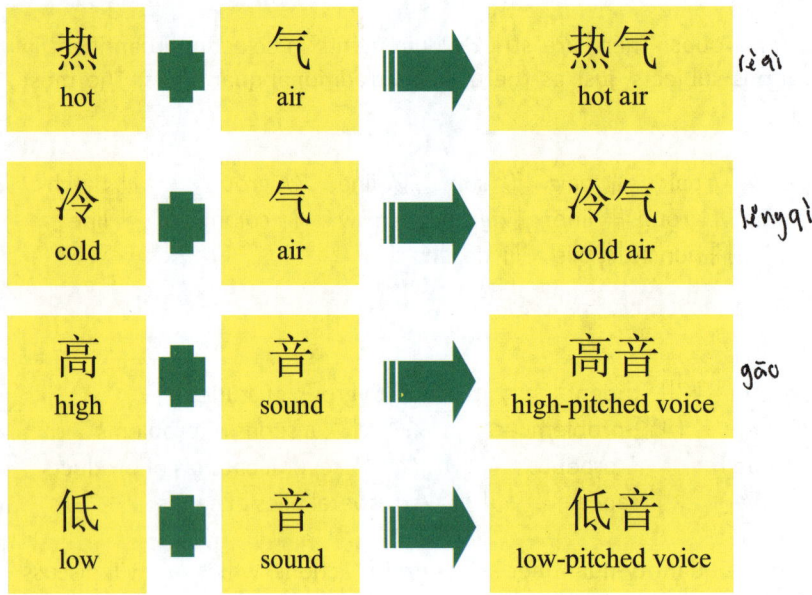

This is a very common and productive method of creating vocabulary words. People can create such words flexibly as long as it is reasonable to combine the characters. In most cases, such words are temporary words, which mean that few of them are included as independent nouns in the dictionary. Other examples:

长 long + 裤 pants, trousers ---- 长裤 trousers chángkù
短 short + 裤 pants, trousers ---- 短裤 shorts
大 big + 雨 rain ---- 大雨 dàyǔ
中 middle + 雨 rain ---- 中雨 zhōngyǔ
小 small + 雨 rain ---- 小雨 xiǎoyǔ
红 red + 灯 light ---- 红灯 red light
绿 green + 灯 light ---- 绿灯 green light
黄 yellow + 灯 light ---- 黄灯 yellow light

Case 2:

The second case is also interesting. The following example helps explain the basic mechanism.

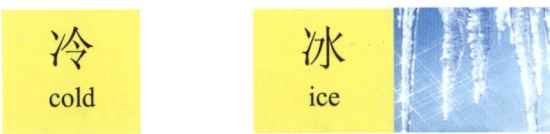

The character 冷 (cold) contains only a vague idea about "coldness," while 冰 (ice) brings a more exact idea of how cold something is. Therefore, when the two characters are combined they produce a new word that describes a state in a more explicit way, like the abbreviation for saying *as cold as ice*.

Most such combinations are fixed words and must be memorized. In these cases, it is not a good idea to create new ones even if it seems reasonable to do so. Other examples:

火 fire + 热 hot ---- 火热 fiery-hot
火 fire + 红 red ---- 火红 fiery-red
雪 snow + 白 white ---- 雪白 snow-white
雪 snow + 亮 bright ---- 雪亮 shiny
绵 cotton + 软 soft ---- 绵软 as soft as cotton

Note: 一般 or 一样 is popularly used to construct a phrase as a trope. For example:

火 fire + 一样 + 热 hot ---- 火一样热 as hot as fire
玉 jade + 一般 + 润 sleek ---- 玉一般润 as sleek as jade

Comparing:

雪白 and 白雪：雪白 means *as white as snow,* and 白雪 means *white snow*. This is not a useless word today. We have already heard news reports of 黑雪 caused by serious pollution.

Case 3:

The above two types of characters can also be combined to emphasize a specific feature of an object. In this case, the character for state should be put at the end of the combination, and it should be regarded as a word referring to a specific state. For example:

Chapter 3 Basic Rules for Combining Words

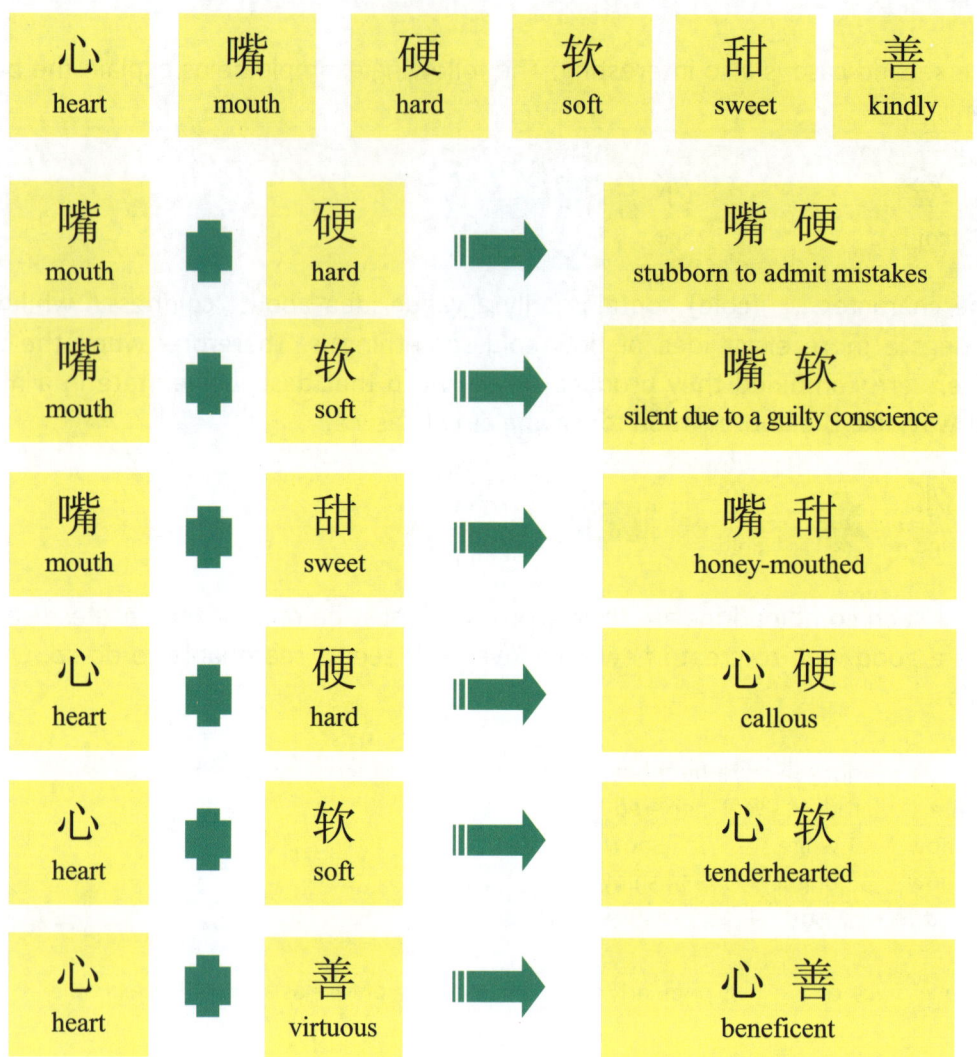

Chapter 3 Basic Rules for Combining Words

Extra Knowledge: Homophones and Polyphones

A popular phenomenon of the Chinese language is that many Chinese characters share one pronunciation. For example:

[yī]: 一 衣 依 医 伊 揖 铱 咿
[yí]: 夷 姨 仪 移 颐 疑 沂 宜 彝 遗
[yǐ]: 已 以 矣 苡 迤 蚁 倚 旖
[yì]: 亿 易 益 翼 译 艺 抑 抑 役 臆 逸 疫 裔 意 毅

It also happens in combinations:

[yì tóng]:   一同 together   异同 variety
[yù yán]:   预言 prediction   寓言 allegory
[píng dìng]: 平定 pacification 评定 to evaluate
[bō lí]:   玻璃 glass   剥离 to peel

Homophones do not lead to misunderstanding in their written form, nor do they when spoken due to the influence of the context. At the same time, some Chinese characters have several pronunciations denoting different meanings. For example:

便   方便[fāng biàn] convenient 便宜[pián yi] cheap
恶   恶劣[è liè] execrable   恶心[ě xīn] sick   厌恶[yàn wù] to detest
和   和平[hé píng] peace   附和[fù hè] to echo   搅和[jiǎo huó] to spoil

When it is hard to create an exact word combination for a new subject that comes from another culture, people usually integrate the characters with the corresponding pronunciations to imitate the subject's original pronunciation. For example:

radar   laser   engine
雷达[léi dá]   镭射[léi shè]   引擎[yǐn qíng]

In the Chinese language, people also use characters to imitate some sounds regardless of the characters' actual meanings. For example:

当[dāng]   轰[hōng]   呼[hū]   咚[dōng]

Meanwhile, some characters are frequently used in written form for various exclamations. Here are the frequently used ones:

唉[ài]   啊[ā]   哼[hēng]   哦[ē]   呀[yā]   哎[èi]   呦[yōu]   哇[wā]   啦[lā]

031

Section 3: Where Both Words Refer to States

Two characters that both refer to state can also be combined to create a new word. There are three basic cases for such combinations.

Case 1:

Two characters both referring to the same (or almost the same) state and the combination comes out with the same meaning. This is the same mechanism as when combining two characters that both refer to the same object. For example:

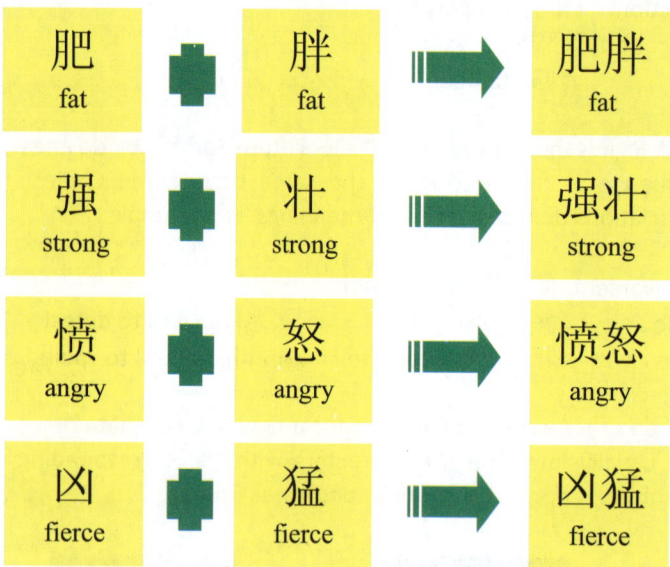

Note: In English grammar, the suffix is frequently used to turn an adjective into an adverb, while some words function both as an adjective and an adverb. However, in Chinese, most words can function as both an adjective and an adverb.

There are numerous basic words for state in the Chinese language. So many, in fact, that there is almost no margin left for users to create new ones. Other examples include:

柔 soft + 软 soft ---- 柔软 soft
强 hard + 硬 hard ---- 强硬 hard
迅 rapid; rapidly + 速 rapid; rapidly ---- 迅速 rapid; rapidly
缓 slow; slowly + 慢 slow; slowly ---- 缓慢 slow; slowly
遥 far + 远 far ---- 遥远 far, remote
明 bright + 亮 bright ---- 明亮 bright, shining
庞 giant + 大 large, big ---- 庞大 giant, large, big
美 beautiful + 丽 pretty ---- 美丽 nice, beautiful

Chapter 3 Basic Rules for Combining Words

Case 2:

When two characters referring to opposite states are combined, they come out with a word referring to a universal concept, which should be regarded as a word for an abstract object. For example:

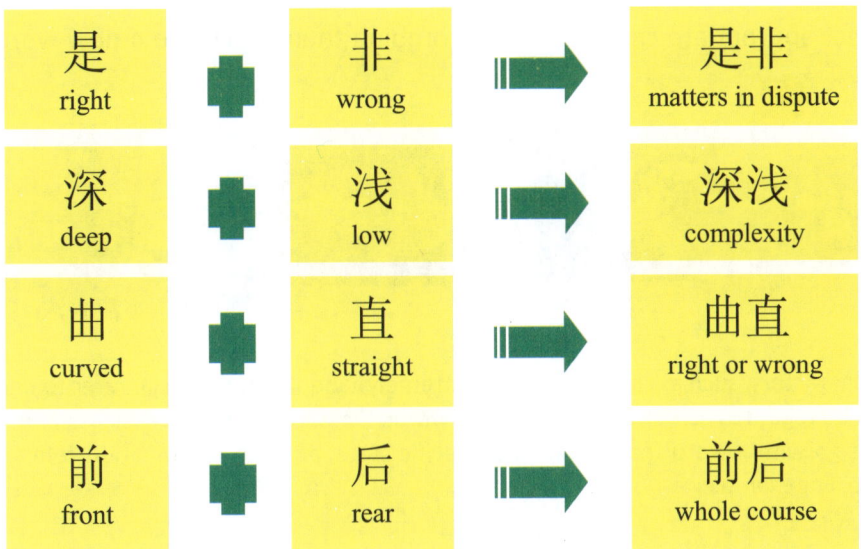

Most of these words are already fixed and there is little margin left for creating new ones. Other examples include:

大 big + 小 small ---- 大小 dimension, size
上 up + 下 down ---- 上下 fluctuation, collectivity
内 inside + 外 outside ---- 内外 the whole range
冷 cold + 暖 warm ---- 冷暖 changes of temperature
好 good + 坏 bad ---- 好坏 stand or fall; character
轻 light + 重 heavy ---- 轻重 weight, degree
好 good + 歹 bad ---- 好歹 anyhow; mishap
方 square + 圆 round ---- 方圆 circumference

Case 3:

In this case, two characters referring to various states can be combined to create a new word as long as they provide an appropriate description of the features of the new subject. Logic and reasoning work well in this case, and we have considerable freedom in creating new words in conversation. Most such combinations, however, are usually temporary words. For example, the following characters are often used to describe food:

Chapter 3 Basic Rules for Combining Words

 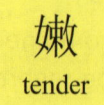   软 soft

香 tasty　嫩 tender　浓 thick　爽 cool　软 soft　甜 sweet

We can select appropriate characters and combine them to create a new word to describe food:

香浓

爽嫩

香软

爽甜香浓

Note: Some characters, such as 很 (very), 极 (extremely) and 太 (too, very), refer to degree or extent, and can be regarded as a special category of words for states. In most cases, such characters should always go with a word that refers to a specific state, and the combination refers to a more specific state. For example:

很 very + 甜 sweet ---- 很甜 very sweet
挺 quite + 香 tasty ---- 挺香 quite tasty
特 very + 好 good ---- 特好 very good
太 too + 差 bad ---- 太差 too bad
极 extremely + 快 fast ---- 极快 extremely fast

In most cases, the above two types of characters can be combined freely as needed, and almost all such combinations are for temporary use. Thus, we do not regard these combinations as a typical example of the rule of combining characters to create new words.

 Quick Reference:

Here is a list of the most frequently used words to describe degree or extent.

很, 非常, 特别	very	最, 极	extremely, most
十分, 挺	very, quite	有些, 有一些	a little
太	too	稍, 稍微	a little; slightly
有点, 有一点	a little	略, 略微, 稍微	appreciably
绝对	absolutely	格外	especially
极, 极其	extraordinarily	相当	quite, rather

Chapter 3 Basic Rules for Combining Words

 Extra Knowledge: Names in Chinese

In Chinese, a person's name usually includes a **surname** and a **given name**. Most names include two or three characters. A surname comes from one's parents (**in most cases from the father**) and typically includes one character. According to statistics, the most widely used surnames are 李, 王, 张, 刘, 陈 and 杨. Sometimes you can find surnames with two characters, such as 上官, 西门, 东方, 尉迟, 司徒 and 司马, etc.

A given name usually includes one or two characters. It is very important for a family to select the appropriate characters for a newborn. People always try to find the characters that can carry their wishes and blessings for a new life. This also happens when people give names to new things, such as buildings, companies, workshops, etc.

In the Chinese tradition, some characters are frequently used in the given name.

Examples for females:

秀 兰 瑜 花 美 玉 芹 灵 芝 妍 洁 香 丽 荔 丹 灵 香

Examples for males:

强 刚 壮 杰 阳 志 伟 山 钢 峰 名 明 长 富 盛 猛 柱

For brothers or sisters, a family selects a common character in their given names as a mark for a specific generation in a clan. For example:

周晓更　周晓恒　周晓平

The characters in a name also have meaning, and people aim to make the combination itself significant.

白雪　周游　常胜　游历

Chapter 3 Basic Rules for Combining Words

Section 4: Where Both Words Refer to Actions

Characters referring to actions can also be combined to create new words in three cases.

Case 1:

The two characters refer to the same (or almost the same) action and the combination of the two characters produces a word with the same meaning. For example:

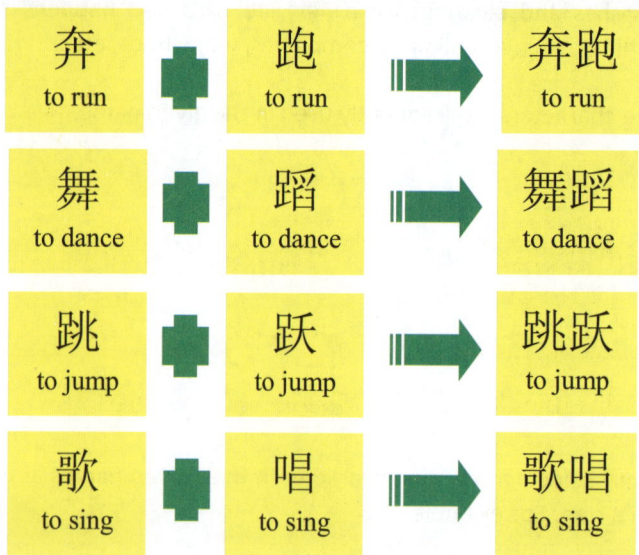

Most of these types of words are fixed and there is little margin for creating new ones. Other examples include:

阅 to read + 读 to read ---- 阅读 to read
观 to watch, to look + 看 ---- 观看 to watch, to look
评 to comment + 论 to comment ---- 评论 to comment
偷 to steal + 盗 to steal ---- 偷盗 to steal, to pilfer
打 to hit + 击 to knock ---- 打击 to hit
抵 to resist + 抗 to resist ---- 抵抗 to resist
检 to check + 查 to examine ---- 检查 to examine
清 to clean up + 理 to pack ---- 清理 to clean, to clear

Case 2:

When two characters that refer to opposite actions are combined, they usually produce a word referring to a mixture of actions or a typical action, or both.

For example:

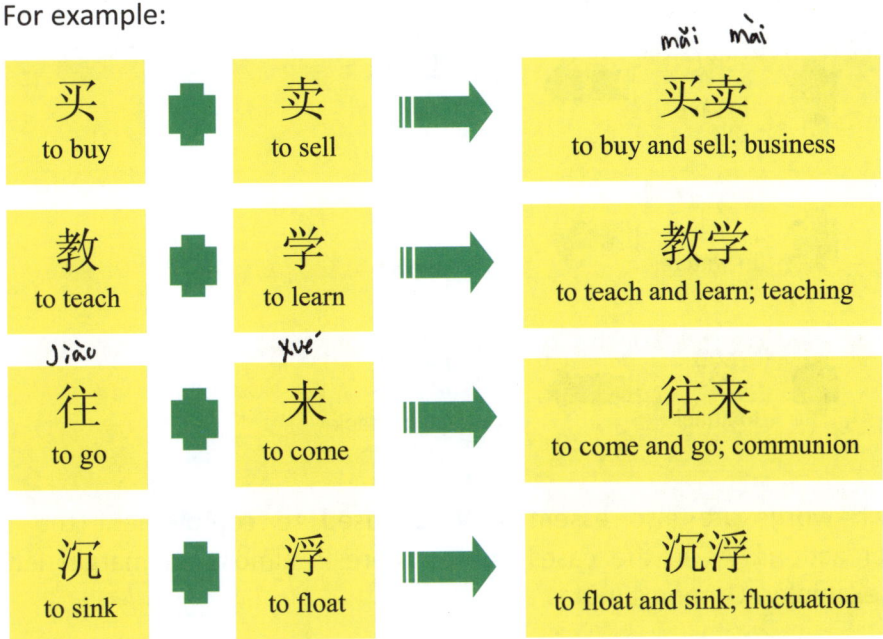

Most such words are fixed with little margin for creating new ones. Other examples:

进 to advance + 退 to retreat ---- 进退 to advance and retreat; possible actions
取 to take + 舍 to abandon ---- 取舍 to take and abandon; to make a choice
视 to watch + 听 to listen ---- 视听 to watch and listen; observation
收 to collect + 支 to spend ---- 收支 to collect and spend; flow of money
聚 to gather + 散 to part ---- 聚散 to meet and part
离 to part + 合 to joint ---- 离合 to part and joint
好 to like + 恶 to dislike ---- 好恶 taste
起 to rise + 落 to fall ---- 起落 to rise and fall; fluctuation

Note: the meanings of such words can sometimes differ considerably from the meanings of the original characters. For example:

开 to open + 关 to close ---- 开关 to switch
出 to leave + 入 to enter ---- 出入 to leave and enter; discrepancy

Case 3:

In some cases, two actions that are different from each other but happen simultaneously, or in a certain logical sequence, can be regarded as an integrated and independent action. By combining the characters referring to the actions in a logical sequence, we create a new word for that integrated action. Examples:

Chapter 3 Basic Rules for Combining Words

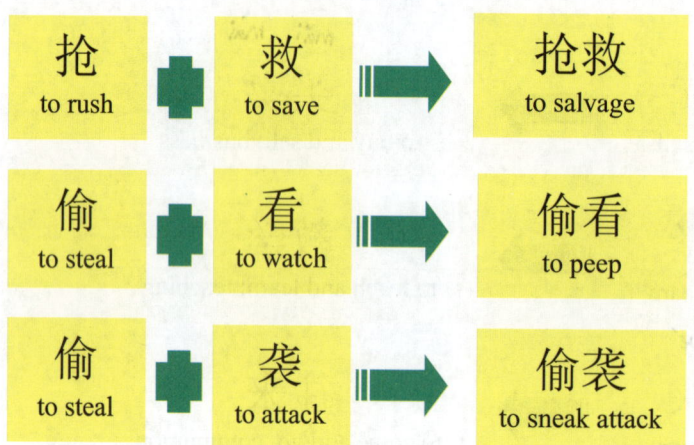

Most such words are also essential words used to complement the basic vocabulary for actions. As in the cases above, there is almost no margin left for creating new examples. Other examples:

搜 to search + 救 to rescue ---- 搜救 to search and rescue
修 to repair + 整 to pack ---- 修整 to repair and pack
救 to save + 助 to help ---- 救助 to save and help
查 to check + 收 to accept ---- 查收 to check and accept
检 to check + 修 to repair ---- 检修 to check and repair
清 to clean up + 扫 to sweep ---- 清扫 to sweep up
整 to pack + 治 to manage ---- 整治 to punish, to renovate
扫 to whisk + 描 to portray ---- 扫描 to scan

 Key Application: Quantity-Quantifier Structure for Actions

We have already discussed the basic application of the quantity-quantifier structure, and the ways this structure can be used to describe a specific action. The quantifiers for action can be categorized as follows:

1. The most commonly used universal quantifiers include:

Quantifier	Function	Examples
次	most commonly used, same with "number of time" in English	试两次 to try several times 检查三次 to check three times

Chapter 3 Basic Rules for Combining Words

下	same with 次	跳几下 to jump several times 试两下 to try several times
遍	for a whole process of an action	说几遍 to speak several times 唱三遍 to sing three times
趟	for the action related with walking, running, moving	来两趟 to come several times 去一趟 to go somewhere one time
顿	for an complete course of an action	打一顿 to beat somebody one time 吃一顿 to have a big meal
阵	implying that an action goes for a while	想一阵 to think for a while 坐一阵 to sit for a while
遭	a slang for 遍, 趟	走一遭 to go somewhere one time

2. Using quantifiers indicating a specific body part used for actions, we can create expressions according to specific situations. For example:

看 to look + 一 one + 眼 eye ---- 看一眼 to have a glance
打 to hit + 几 several + 拳 clench ---- 打几拳 to hit with clenched fist several times
踢 to kick + 一 one + 脚 foot ---- 踢一脚 to give a kick
喊 to shout + 几 several + 嗓子 throat ---- 喊几嗓子 to shout out several times
拍 to clap + 一 one + 巴掌 palm ---- 拍一巴掌 to give applause or clap
戳 to poke + 一 one + 指头 finger ---- 戳一指头 to give a poke with a finger

3. Quantifiers indicating the specific tools for actions. In theory, we have numerous quantifiers of this type. For example:

放 to issue + 几 several + 枪 gun ---- 放几枪 to shoot several times
敲 to knock + 两 two + 棍子 cane ---- 敲两棍子 to knock with a cane several times
喝 to drink + 几 several + 杯 cup ---- 喝几杯 to drink several cups
吃 to eat + 两 two + 盘 dish ---- 吃两盘 to have two dishes (of food)

Chapter 3 Basic Rules for Combining Words

 Extra Knowledge: Chinese Calligraphy

Along with the evolution of Chinese characters, the development of calligraphy also changed in ways that characterize different historical periods.

甲骨文		These characters appeared 5,000 years ago and they are like abstract paintings of the objects they represent.
金鼎文	These characters were found on bells and cooking vessels used about 3,000 years ago. The strokes function more as symbols than pictures.	
石鼓文		About 2,200 years ago, China was united into a single nation with a standard writing style for characters that used fewer strokes and had a fixed internal structure.
隶书	About 2,000 years ago, a more practical and efficient typeset was created, making writing more quickly and easily. This is the foundation of modern characters.	
楷书		Since then, people pursuing an aesthetic value to writing. 楷书 established the basic rules of calligraphy that are still widely used today.
行书	行书 is popularly used in daily handwriting. Compared with 楷书, it is slightly cramped, which guarantees quick writing.	
草书		As the art of calligraphy developed, 草书 appeared. Though it has little practical function, it is very important in the art of Chinese calligraphy.

Chapter 3 Basic Rules for Combining Words

Section 5: Where Words Refer to Objects and Actions

A character referring to an action can also be combined with a character referring to an object. There are seven main cases of this type of combination:

Case 1:

Sometimes, there is a direct relation between an action and an object, which is interpreted as "an action directly influences an object" or "an object is the target of the action". In this case, the combination usually refers to a more specific action. For example:

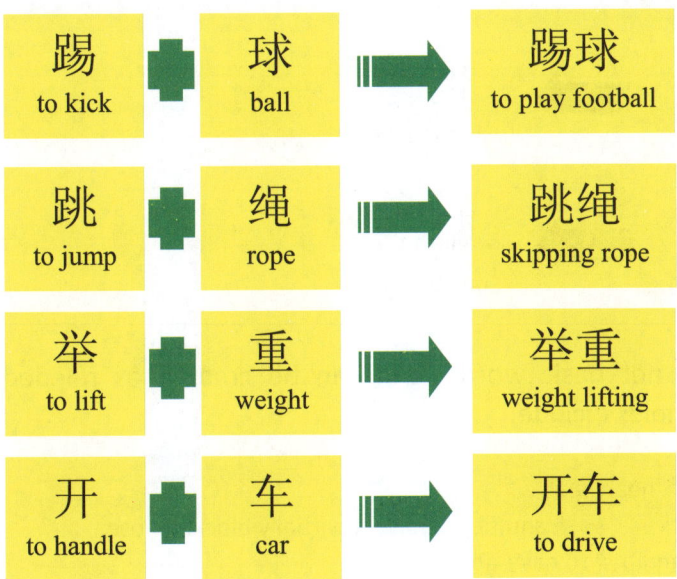

Only parts of these kinds of words are basic words. We can create such words in everyday speech, as long as it is reasonable to combine the two types of characters. More examples include:

充 to fill, to charge + 气 gas, air ---- 充气 to inflate
充 to fill, to charge + 电 electricity ---- 充电 to electrify
喝 to drink + 酒 wine, alcohol ---- 喝酒 to drink liquor
探 to explore, to scout + 险 danger ---- 探险 to explore, to adventure
玩 to play + 牌 cards ---- 玩牌 to play cards
打 to hit, to play + 针 needle ---- 打针 to take an injection
扫 to sweep, to whisk + 地 floor ---- 扫地 to sweep the floor
洗 to wash + 衣 clothes ---- 洗衣 to wash clothes

041

Chapter 3 Basic Rules for Combining Words

Case 2:

These two types of characters can also be combined to create a word referring to a specific action by an object. Sometimes, such words also refer to specific phenomena. In this case, the sequence of characters is different to that in Case 1. For example:

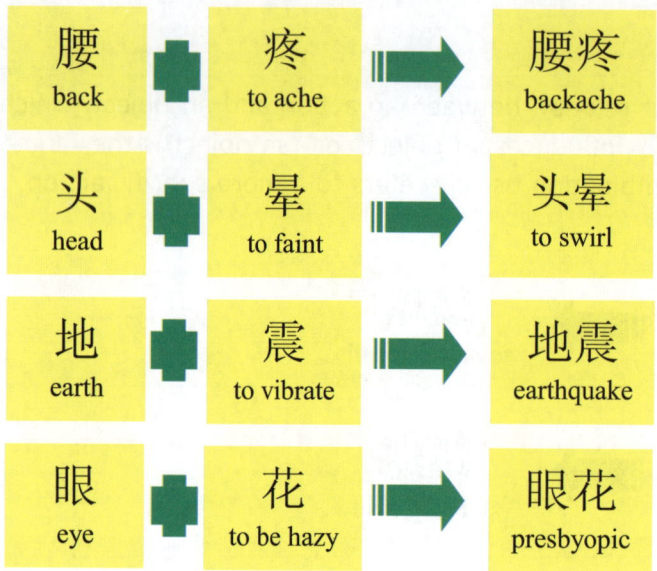

Most of such words are not basic words, and can be created as needed in everyday speaking. Other examples include:

心 heart + 跳 to beat ---- 心跳 heartbeat
鼻 nose + 塞 to choke, to block ---- 鼻塞 snuffle; to have a partially blocked nose
耳 ear + 鸣 to ring ---- 耳鸣 tinnitus; to have tinnitus
腹 abdomen + 泻 to effuse, to outpour ---- 腹泻 diarrhea; to have diarrhea
海 sea + 啸 to howl ---- 海啸 tsunami
日 sun + 蚀 to corrode, to erode ---- 日蚀 solar eclipse
月 moon + 蚀 to corrode, to erode ---- 月蚀 lunar eclipse
尘 dust + 暴 to erupt ---- 尘暴 dust devil

Case 3:

These two types of characters can also be combined to create a new word for a specific action implying that "an action is performed with the help of a tool or in a certain method". Examples:

042

Chapter 3 Basic Rules for Combining Words

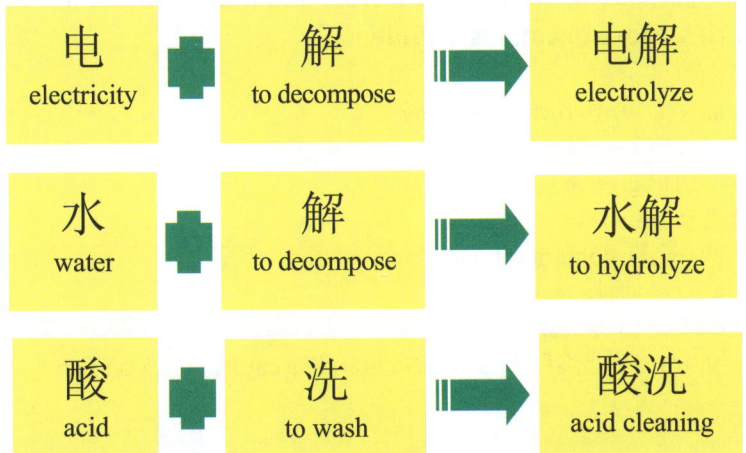

Most such words are basic words in the vocabulary. Other examples include:

电 electricity + 离 to separate ---- 电离 to ionize; ionization
电 electricity + 动 to drive ---- 电动 (to be) driven by electricity
气 air, gas + 动 to drive ---- 气动 (to be) driven by pneumatic power
水 water + 溶 to dissolve, to melt ---- 水解 to dissolve with water
水 water + 冷 to cool, to refrigerate ---- 水冷 to water-cool
气 air, gas + 冷 to cool, to refrigerate ---- 气冷 to air-cool
热 heat + 熔 to melt, to fuse ---- 热熔 to melt by heat
胶 glue + 合 to join, to combine ---- 胶合 to adhere or to be glued together

Case 4:

These two types of characters also can be combined to create a word for a specific object, indicating that the object is a result of certain influences. For example:

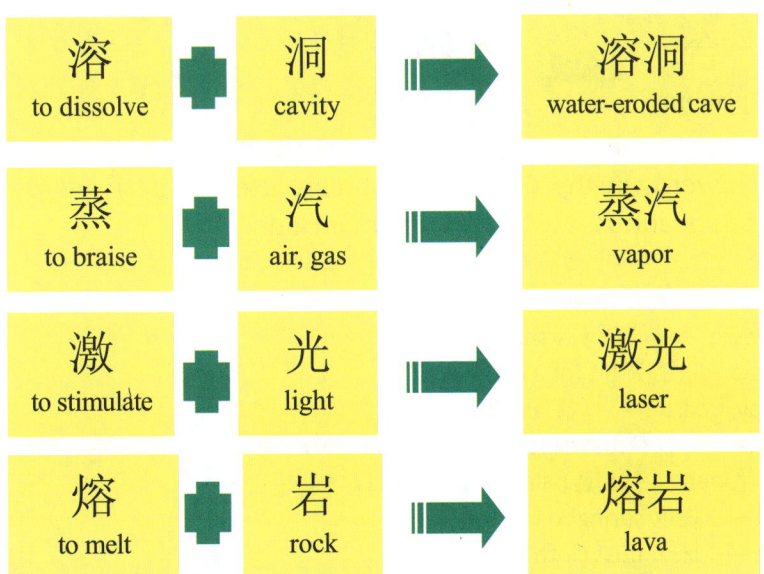

Chapter 3 Basic Rules for Combining Words

Most of these words are already fixed as basic words, and a lot of them are used as jargon for specific industries. More examples include:

裂 to crack, to split + 缝 gap ---- 裂缝 crevasse, cranny
焊 to weld + 缝 gap, trail ---- 焊缝 welding line
切 to cut + 口 gap, nick ---- 切口 groove cut
切 to cut + 线 line ---- 切线 tangent
交 to intersect + 点 point ---- 交点 point of intersection
划 to scrape + 痕 mark, trace ---- 划痕 nick
伤 to injure + 痕 mark, trace ---- 伤痕 scar
烙 to cauterize + 印 imprint, trace ---- 烙印 brand (as in branding cattle), mark on skin

Case 5:

The two types of characters listed below are frequently combined to create new words for objects with specific functions, or objects for the performance of specific actions. For example:

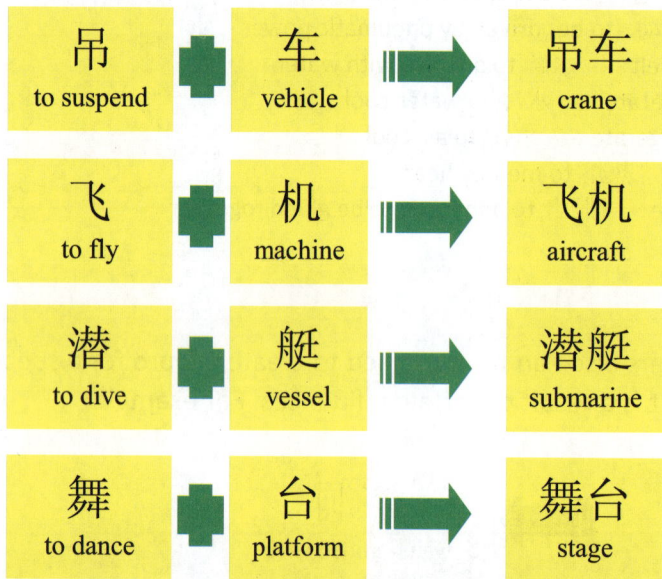

There are many such words in the Chinese vocabulary used as basic words for items, tools, machines and apparatuses. Other examples include:

铲 to shovel + 车 vehicle ---- 铲车 forklift
战 to fight + 船 ship, vessel ---- 战船 warship
钻 to drill + 头 head, top ---- 钻头 bit (of a drill)
算 to calculate + 盘 tray, board ---- 算盘 abacus
饮 to drink + 料 material ---- 饮料 beverage
画 to paint, to draw + 笔 pen ---- 画笔 paintbrush
跳 to jump + 板 board ---- 跳板 springboard
抹 to smear + 布 cloth ---- 抹布 dust cloth

Chapter 3 Basic Rules for Combining Words

Note: The mechanism in Case 5 can be extended to more universal situations. For example:

拉 to pull + 手 hand ----拉手 handle of a door, window, etc.
提 to lift + 手 hand ----提手 handle of a suitcase, box, etc.
护 to protect + 膝 knee ---- 护膝 knee pad
护 to protect + 腕 wrist ----护腕 cuff

Case 6:

These two types of characters can also be combined to create words for specific categories of people. In this case, one character usually refers to people and the other refers to a typical action of people. For example:

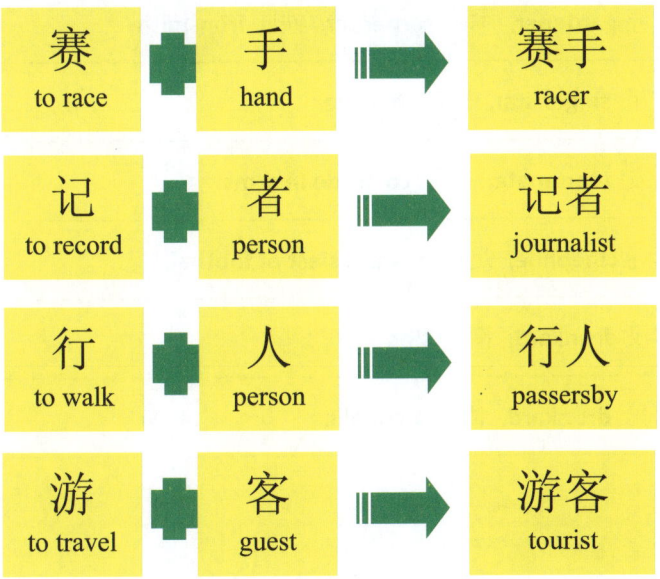

In this case, some characters are used frequently in the combinations:

人	human, people	男人 man/men, 女人 woman/women, 工人 worker
者	person, personnel	学者 scholar, 患者 patient
员	member	学员 learner, 船员 sailor
客	guest	顾客 customer, 访客 visitor
士	person	战士 soldier, 护士 nurse, 学士 bachelor
生	learner	学生 student, 考生 examinee

Chapter 3 Basic Rules for Combining Words

手	hand	水手 sailor, 对手 adversary, 枪手 gunner
家	master	画家 artist (painting), 作家 author, 科学家 scientist
师	instructor	教师 teacher, 厨师 chef, 律师 lawyer
长	administrator	家长 householder, 船长 captain of a ship, 班长 monitor
工	worker	木工 carpenter, 电工 electrician, 技工 artisan
匠	craftsman	花匠 gardener, 木匠 carpenter, 铁匠 ironsmith
星	star	歌星 singer star, 影星 film star
友	friend	队友 teammate, 战友 comrade in arms
迷	enthusiast	影迷 cinephile, 足球迷 enthusiast of football
汉	man	醉汉 drunkard, 懒汉 slob
鬼	ghost	醉鬼 drunkard, 酒鬼 alcoholic

Case 7:

By combining a character referring to an animal with a character referring to its typical action, we can get a word referring to a more explicit action. This is also a way to create a trope. For example:

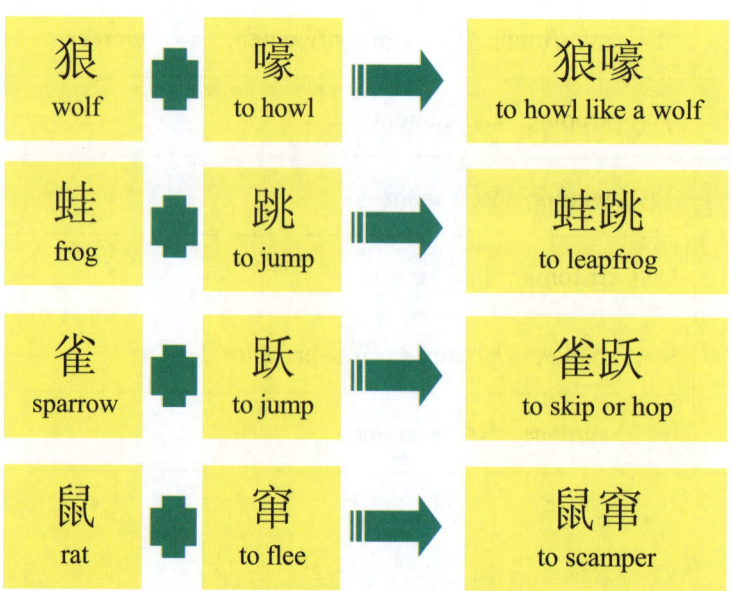

Chapter 3 Basic Rules for Combining Words

 Key Application: Expressing Numbers

Chinese has corresponding characters for Arabic numbers. In business, people use these characters to prevent misunderstandings. You can easily find them in contracts or invoices.

0	1	2	3	4	5	6	7	8	9
零	一	二	三	四	五	六	七	八	九
零	壹	贰	叁	肆	伍	陆	柒	捌	玖

The popular units for numbers are:

十 ten　百 hundred　千 thousand　万 ten thousand　亿 a hundred million

1. Expressing a cardinal number

In the Chinese language, people used to divide long numbers every four digits, and then place the numbers before the corresponding units. The following example shows the basic mechanism involved:

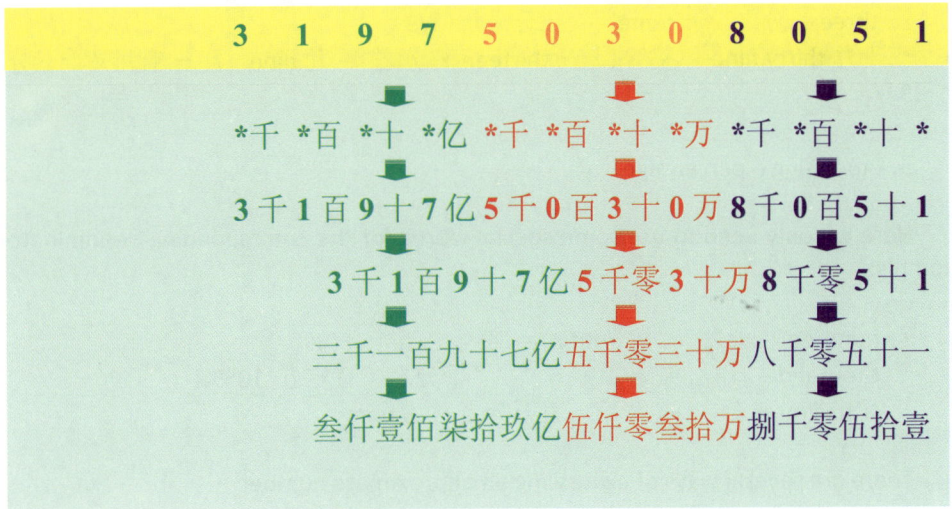

2. Expressing an ordinal number

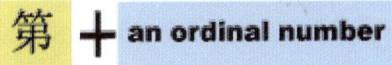 an ordinal number

第 +

Examples:

第 + 一 one ---- 第一 first
第 + 二 two ---- 第二 second
第 + 五十六 fifty six ---- 第五十六 the fifty sixth

047

第 + 一万零三百七十五 ten thousand three hundred seventy five ---- 第一万零三百七十五 the ten thousand three hundred seventy fifth

3. Expressing a number with a decimal fraction

expression for the integer part **+ 点 +** corresponding characters for the numbers in decimal part

Examples:

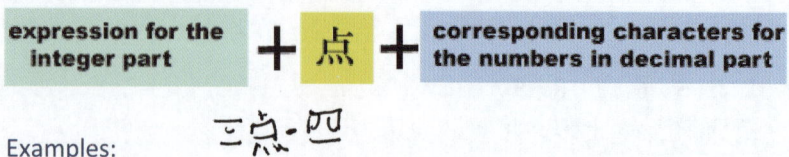

三 three + 点 + 一四 1, 4 ---- 三点一四 3.14
一万六千零八 sixteen thousand and eight + 点 + 零六 0, 6 ---- 一万六千零八点零六 16008.06

4. Expressing a number with a fraction

expression for the integer part **+ 又 +** expression for the number as a denominator **+ 分之 +** expression for the number as a numerator

Examples:

三 three + 分之 + 一 one ---- 三分之一 1/3
三十九 thirty nine + 又 + 十三 thirteen + 分之 + 九 nine ---- 三十九又十三分之九 39 9/13

5. Expressing a percentage

Here we only need to use some special words for the corresponding denominators. Examples:

百 hundred + 分之 + 五十 fifty ---- 百分之五十 50%
千 thousand + 分之 + 一百零五 ---- 千分之一百零五 105‰
百万 million + 分之 + 六 ---- 百万分之六 6 ppm

There are several ways of expressing an approximate number.

1. We can use some special characters like 多, 几, 数, 左右, 上下, 来 to substitute a number not specified. For example:

几 several + 十 ten ---- 几十 tens of
数 several + 百 hundred ---- 数百 hundreds of
一百 one hundred + 多 ---- 一百多 more than one hundred
三千六百 three thousand six hundred + 左右 ---- 三千六百左右 around three thousand six hundred
六十 sixty + 上下 ---- 六十上下 around sixty

Chapter 3 Basic Rules for Combining Words

Note: 来 is also frequently used in these expressions and, in most cases, it should be used in a quantity-quantifier structure. For example:

十 ten + 来 + 个 ---- 十来个 around ten
一百 a hundred + 来 + 吨 ton ---- 一百来吨 about one hundred tons

2. In spoken language, people usually use two neighboring numbers to represent an approximate quantity. This expression usually goes with a quantity-quantifier structure. For example:

一 one + 两 two + 公斤 kilogram ---- 一两公斤 one or two kilograms
六 six + 七 seven + 个 ---- 六七个 around six
三 three + 四 four + 千 thousand ---- 三四千 about three thousand

In addition, 把 (把来) is usually added after 百, 千, 万 to express an approximate quantity. For example:

百 hundred + 把 + 本 + 书 ---- 百把本书 around one hundred books
千 thousand + 把来 + 头 + 牛 cow ---- 千把来头牛 about one thousand cows
万 ten thousand + 把来 + 块 + 砖 brick ---- 万把来块砖 about ten thousands bricks

67个 ~6
34千 ~3000

Chapter 3 Basic Rules for Combining Words

Section 6: Where Words Refer to States and Actions

Many characters are used for specific states, such as 快 (fast), 慢 (slowly), 高 (highly) and 低 (lowly), etc. Such characters are frequently combined with the characters referring to actions. There are three main cases of this type of combination:

Case 1:

This mechanism is best illustrated by an example. A bird can fly (飞) in various states, such as 快 (fast), 慢 (slowly), 高 (highly) and 低 (lowly). These two types of characters can be combined as a word referring to a more specific action:

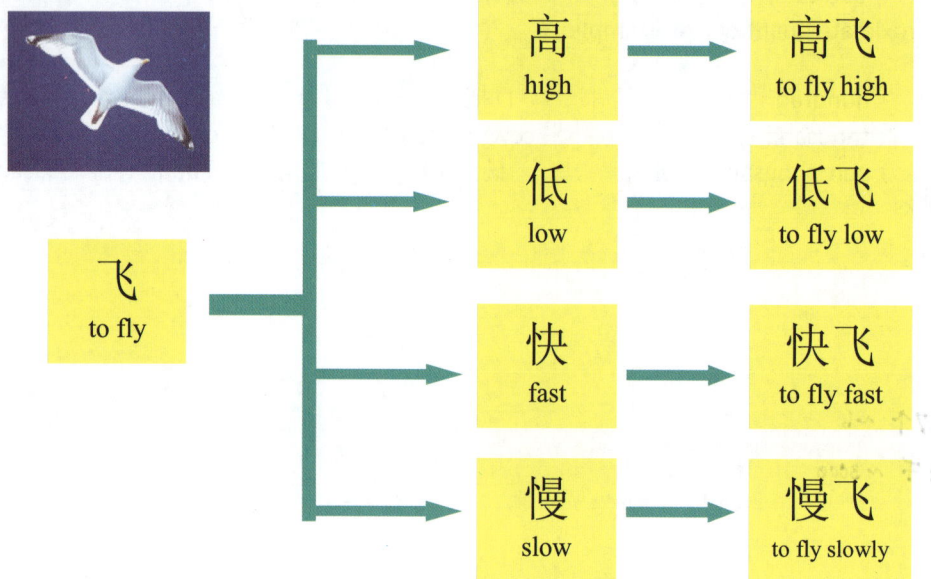

Sometimes, the meanings of the words are quite different from what they appear to be. Examples:

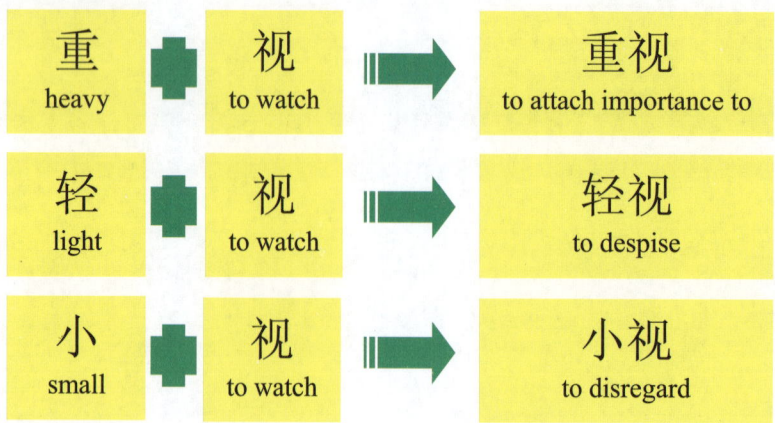

Chapter 3 Basic Rules for Combining Words

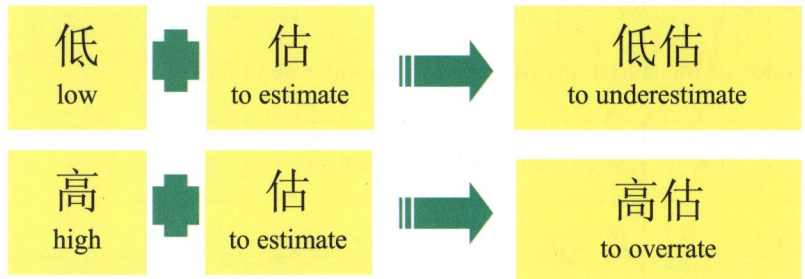

Case 2:

The combination of these two types of characters can also indicate that an action happens in a specific fashion, or ends in a specific state. In this case, the character referring to the state should be put at the end of the combination. For example:

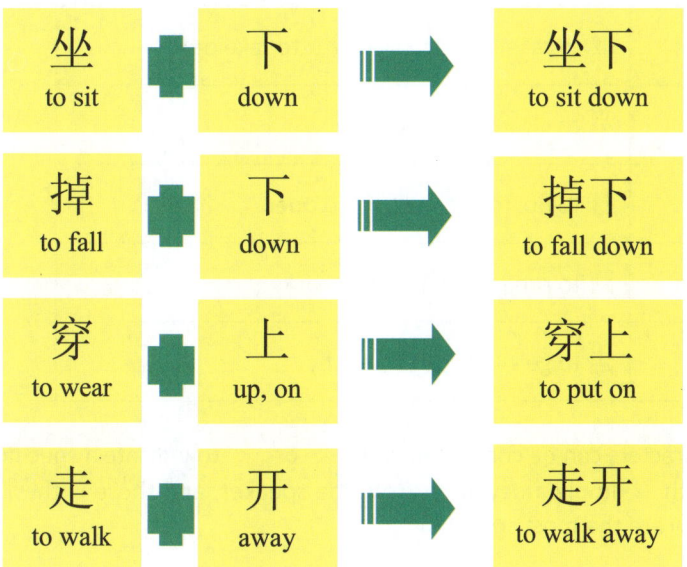

We can make such combinations freely as required. Some characters referring to states are frequently used in making such combinations.

Case 3:

To create a word with a more explicit state, we can combine two types of characters to produce a trope. For example:

051

Chapter 3 Basic Rules for Combining Words

 Key Application: List of Characters

Here is a collection of the characters that are frequently used in Case 2.

上	up, on, upon	戴 to wear----戴上 to put on
下	down	放 to put ----放下 to put down
来	in	出----出来 to come out
去	out, away	去 to go----拿去 to take away
进	in, into	放 to put ----放进 to put in, to put into
出	out, away	取 to take, to fetch ----取出 to take out
起	up, upon	举 to lift ----举起 to lift up
开	out, away	打 to do, to act----打开 to open
回	back, around	跑 to run ----跑回 to run back
过	by	走 to go ----走过 to pass by

Most of the above characters can be composed with 去 or 来 to indicate a specific trend. Those composed with 去 imply a deviation from the speaker, and those with 来 imply a reverse trend. Below are the most common:

	上	下	进	出	回	开	过	起
来	上来	下来	进来	出来	回来	开来	过来	起来
去	上去	下去	进去	出去	回去	开去	过去	---

We can combine them the same as we did previously. For example:

爬上来 to climb up 　　爬进去 to climb into
躺下来 to lie down 　　躺上去 to lie on (something)
走回去 to walk back into 　　走过来 to walk toward
说出去 to speak out (to others) 　　说出来 to speak out

In addition to the above applications, this structure is also frequently used to emphasize the repetition of an action:

action + 来 + action + 去

Examples:

走 to walk: 走来走去 to walk around; to wander
想 to think: 想来想去 to surmise for quite a time
翻 to turn, 覆 to turn: 翻来覆去 to toss and turn
颠 to turn, 倒 to turn: 颠来倒去 to do something over and over

 Extra Knowledge: Diverse Meanings of a Combination

Most characters are usually flexible in their meaning and this trait makes them powerful and flexible when combined with other characters. At the same time, the process of combining characters should proceed logically. It is possible to combine two characters using a different logical approach but this will result in a different meaning. For example:

Here are the basic meanings of 热:
1. heat (referring to an act),
2. warm, hot (referring to a temperature state),
3. popular (referring to a state).

We can have a combination 热水 using two types of logic, and it results in different meanings:

热 hot, warm; to heat up
热 hot, warm 水 water 热水 hot water; warm water
热 to heat up 水 water 热水 to heat up the water

Other examples:

跳绳 rope skipping, a kind of sport; a rope especially for the sport
塑像 statue; to make a statue

This means that we have to deduce the exact meaning of a combination of characters according to the specific context.

Section 7: Summary

The previous sections demonstrate the most important cases in the combination of two characters. The principles and rules in these cases are the bedrock of the grammar system. They dominate the creation of the basic vocabulary and influence the construction of phrases and sentences. Please note, however, the cases discussed above only cover the most popular and common in the language.

The vocabulary of the Chinese language has two main categories: one is basic words that are listed as formal lemmas in dictionaries; and temporary words that are constructed as needed in practical language (also defined as complex words). The phrases are a part of the complex words. The following chart shows the differences and relations among the above concepts.

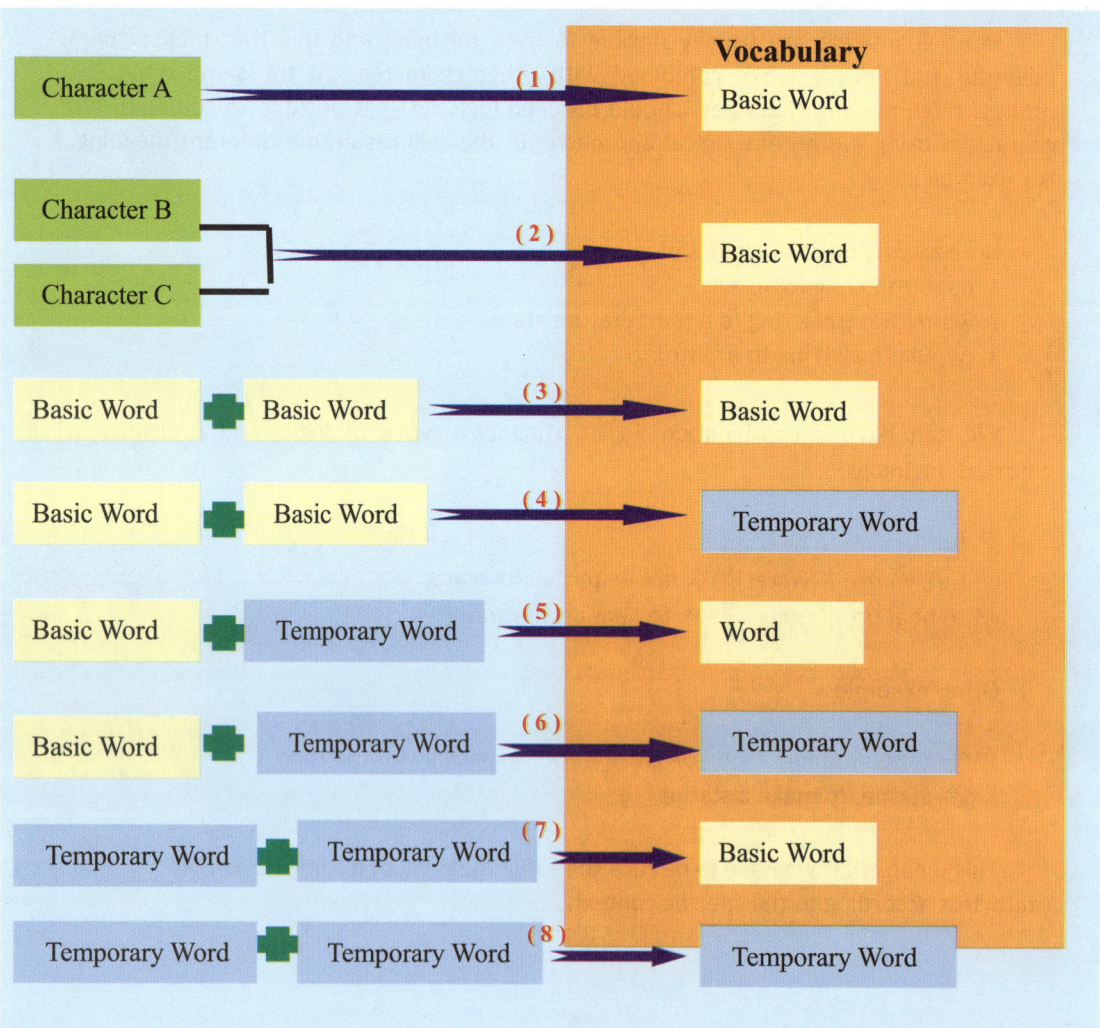

Chapter 3 Basic Rules for Combining Words

There are eight situations in the combination of characters:

(1): In most cases, a character itself is a basic word, corresponding to one or more independent meanings. The individual characters build up the primary words in the vocabulary. For example:

水 water　车 vehicle　天 sky　吃 eat　跑 run　睡 sleep　快 fast　慢 slow　很 very

(2): Sometimes, a character itself means nothing, and must be combined with other character(s) to make sense. This combination is still a basic word. For example:

蝴蝶 butterfly　骆驼 camel　蹒跚 hobble　尴尬 embarrass　枇杷 loquat

(3): Two or more basic words can be further combined to make a new basic word This is the most important method of enlarging the basic vocabulary. For example:

计 to calculate + 算 to calculate ---- 计算 to calculate
电 electricity + 线 line ---- 电线 wire
键 key + 盘 board ---- 键盘 keyboard
计算 to calculate + 机 machine ---- 计算机 computer

(4): A word constructed of two (or more) basic words is usually a complex word (temporary word), and most of these can be regarded as phrases. For example:

喝 to drink + 水 water ---- 喝水 to drink water
修 to repair + 车 vehicle ---- 修车 to repair a vehicle
写 to write + 信 letter ---- 写信 to write a letter
洗 to wash + 衣 clothes ---- 洗衣 to wash clothes

(5): A word constructed by a basic word and a complex word usually results in a basic word. For example:

洗衣 to wash clothes + 机 machine ---- 洗衣机 washing machine
售货 to sell goods + 员 clerk ---- 售货员 salesperson
绘图 to draw a chart + 仪 apparatus ---- 绘图仪 graph plotter
消音 to diminish the noise + 器 apparatus ---- 消音器 silencer

(6): In most cases, a word constructed from a basic word and a complex word is a complex word. This is a major method of creating phrases in everyday speech. For example:

洗衣 to wash clothes + 服务 service ---- 洗衣服务 the laundry service
洗衣服务 the laundry service + 费用 cost, fee ---- 洗衣服务费用 the fee for the laundry service

Chapter 3 Basic Rules for Combining Words

洗衣 to wash clothes + 过程 procedure ---- 洗衣过程 the procedure of washing clothes
正确 correct + 洗衣过程 the procedure of washing clothes ---- 正确的洗衣过程 the correct procedure for washing clothes

Note: In the following chapter, we will discuss details about building complex words in complicated structures.

(7): A word constructed by two (or more) complex words is usually a basic word For example:

隐形 invisible, impossible to be seen + 眼镜片 optical lens ---- 隐形眼镜片 contact lens
浇花 to water the flower + 水壶 water pot ---- 浇花壶 watering can
室内 in the house + 盆栽植物 potted plant ---- 室内盆栽植物 houseplant
停车 to park a car + 收费计 toll meter ---- 停车收费计 parking meter

(8): In most cases, a word constructed by two (or more) complex words is also a complex word or phrase. For example:

经济发展 the development of economy + 整体水平 whole level ---- 经济发展整体水平 the whole level of the development of economy
正常成年人 a normal adult + 学习能力 capability in learning ---- 正常成年人的学习能力 the learning capability of a normal adult
学习汉语 to learn the Chinese language + 最好方法 the best way ---- 学习汉语的最好方法 the best way to learn the Chinese language
打开 to open + 车门 the door of a car ---- 打开车门 to open the door of the car

The key to combining two independent meanings is that they interact with each other in order to generate another independent meaning. Therefore, the examples of the combining cases discussed in the previous six sections can be placed into three types according to their logical features:

Logic Type 1 (LT-1):

Two words (A and B) both referring to the same (or almost the same) meaning are combined to generate a word that refers to the same meaning.

Examples:

策 plan + 略 plan ---- 策略 plan
法 law + 律 regulation ---- 法律 law

赤 red + 红 red ---- 赤红 red
柔 soft + 软 soft ---- 柔软 soft
寻 to look for + 找 to look for ---- 寻找 to look for

Logic Type 2 (LT-2):

Two words (A and B) that refer to opposite meanings are combined to generate a word that refers to the sum total of the category (represented by C).

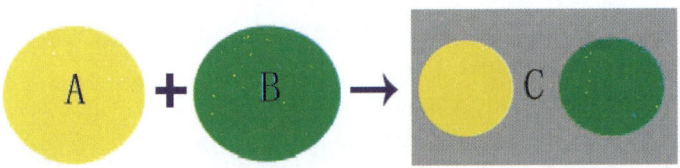

Examples:

日 day + 夜 night ---- 日夜 a whole day; all the time
水 water + 土 soil ---- 水土 natural environment
鸟 bird + 兽 beast ---- 鸟兽 animals
方 square + 圆 round ---- 方圆 circumference
内 inner + 外 outer ---- 内外 inside and outside; whole

Logic Type 3 (LT-3):

Two words (A and B) both refer to the essential features of an independent subject (whether it is a concrete object, an action, a state, or a concept). The combination of these combined characters functions as a new word (represented by C) to define that subject.

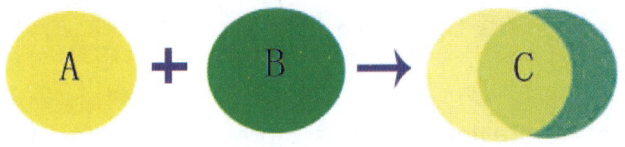

There are several sub-types listed below:

1. A and B have no direct relation (neither in meaning nor in logic) and they both describe the essential features (or properties) of a subject. For example:

项 neck + 链 chain ---- 项链 necklace
手 hand + 机 machine ---- 手机 mobile phone
电 electricity + 话 talk, words ---- 电话 telephone
鞋 shoe + 带 strap ---- 鞋带 bootlace
书 book + 桌 table ---- 书桌 desk

Chapter 3 Basic Rules for Combining Words

2. A describes a specific property of B. For example:

狂 mad + 想 to think ---- 狂想 be rhapsodic
弹 to rebound + 跳 to jump ---- 弹跳 to bounce
蛙 frog + 跳 to jump ---- 蛙跳 to leapfrog
战 to fight + 舰 vessel ---- 战舰 combat vessel
挂 to hang + 钩 hook ---- 挂钩 hook to hang something on

3. A describes the effects or the outcome of B. For example:

打 to fight + 败 to fail ---- 打败 to beat, to defeat
治 to treat + 愈 to recover ---- 治愈 to cure one's health
逃 to escape + 开 away ---- 逃离 to escape; to get away
分 to divide + 开 open ---- 分开 to separate
说 to speak, to say + 明 bright, clear ---- 说明 to explain; explanation, illustration

4. A is the target of B (usually a word referring to an action). For example:

吃 to eat + 饭 meal ---- 吃饭 to have a meal
开 to hold, to open + 会 meeting ---- 开会 to have a meeting
采 to pick + 油 oil ---- 采油 to extract oil
开 to open + 荒 wilderness ---- 开荒 to open up wasteland
射 to launch + 箭 arrow ---- 射箭 archery

5. A (usually a word referring to an action) is issued by B. For example:

骨 bone + 折 to break ---- 骨折 to break; fracture of bone
耳 ear + 鸣 to ring ---- 耳鸣 tinnitus; to have tinnitus
日 sun + 出 out; to rise ---- 日出 sunrise
日 sun + 落 to fall ---- 日落 sunset
音 sound, voice + 爆 to burst, to blast ---- 音爆 sonic boom

All of the 22 cases described in the previous sections can be regarded as specific extensions of the above three basic logic types, and they can be classified into six main categories. Below is a summary of the six categories with a code added for quick reference.

Chapter 3 Basic Rules for Combining Words

Type	Case	Function	Example	Code
two characters, both refer to concrete objects	with same meaning	1. refers to the same meaning 2. refers to the whole class	房屋 海洋	*TT-1*
	with opposite meaning	refers to the whole kind	男女 春秋	*TT-2*
	with different meaning	creates a new word	电力 水力	*TT-3*
one character refers to a concrete object and the other to a state	-----------------	refers to a specific object	冷气 高音	*ST-3*
	-----------------	refers to a more explicit meaning	火热 火红	*TS-3*
	-----------------	refers to a specific feature	嘴硬 心硬	*TS-3*
two characters, both refer to states	with same meaning	refers to the same meaning	肥胖 强壮	*SS-1*
	with opposite meaning	refers to a general concept	是非 深浅	*SS-2*
	with different meaning	refers to mixed features	香甜 浓爽	*SS-3*
two characters, both refer to actions	with same meaning	refers to the same meaning	奔跑 舞蹈	*AA-1*
	with opposite meaning	1. refers to the same 2. refers to the whole class	买卖 教学	*AA-2*
	with different meaning	refers to an integration of acts	抢修 抢救	*AA-3*
one character refers to a concrete object and the other to an action	-----------------	refers to a specific act	踢球 跳绳	*AT-3*
	-----------------	refers to a specific act	腰疼 头晕	*TA-3*
	-----------------	implies tools or methods of an act	电焊 电解	*TA-3*
	-----------------	implies a cause for something	溶洞 蒸汽	*AT-3*
	-----------------	implies a function of something	吊车 飞机	*TA-3*
	-----------------	implies the occupation or the moving state of somebody	行人 记者	*AT-3*
	-----------------	brings a more specific action	狼嚎 蛙跳	*TA-3*
one character refers to a state and the other an action	-----------------	combines randomly to describe a specific action	快飞 高飞	*SA-3*
	-----------------	implies a specific state caused by an act	坐下 穿上	*AS-3*
	-----------------	refers to a more vivid action	飞快	*AS-3*

Chapter 3 Basic Rules for Combining Words

Each code includes three elements:

1. Characters with specific types of meanings (T: thing, S: state, A: action);
2. The combining sequence of the characters;
3. The basic logical type (1: LT-1, 2: LT-2, 3: LT-3, 4: LT-4).

For example, TT-1 implies that two characters, both referring to objects, are combined under LT-1.

By using the above principles and rules, we can combine tens of characters to make a word to denominate any complicated and intricate meaning. That is to say, the principles and rules make it possible to generate an infinite number of words with a very limited quantity of characters.

Note that in this chapter, in order to make things easily understood, all the words used for examples have two characters. Things are not always that easy because a great many words and phrases have very complicated structures.

Chapter 3 Basic Rules for Combining Words

 Extra Knowledge: Special Cases in Constructing a Combination

1. By adopting a character with an exaggerated meaning, we can produce a trope. For example:

万 ten thousand + 里 mile ---- 万里 literal meaning: ten thousand miles; actual meaning: very long, endless

万 ten thousand + 人 people ---- 万人 literal meaning: ten thousand people; actual meaning many people

千 a thousand + 斤 jin ---- 千斤 literal meaning: one thousand jins; actual meaning: very heavy

百 a hundred + 般 way, method ---- 百般 literal meaning: one hundred methods; actual meaning: every method; every way

Applications:

万里 + 长城 the Great Wall ---- 万里长城 the endless Great Wall
万里 + 长空 sky ---- 万里长空 the boundless sky
千斤 + 重担 load ---- 千斤重担 a very heavy load
千斤 + 重任 hard mission ---- 千斤重任 a very hard mission

2. By doubling a character referring a human being or an object, we can create a word with a more fluent pronunciation without changing its meaning. For example:

爷 grandpa ---- 爷爷 grandpa
爸 dad ---- 爸爸 dad
妈 ma ---- 妈妈 ma
弟 younger brother ---- 弟弟 younger brother

This application can also typically be heard when parents talk to their babies. For example:

狗 dog ---- 狗狗 puppy
猫 cat ---- 猫猫 kitty
手 hand ---- 手手 hand
脚 foot ---- 脚脚 foot

3. By doubling a character referring to a state of a certain action, we can create an accentuated meaning. Most of these words are already fixed in the language. For example:

轻 slightly ---- 轻轻 very slightly
重 heavily ---- 重重 very heavily
深 deeply ---- 深深 very deeply
浅 shallowly ---- 浅浅 very shallowly

061

Chapter 3 Basic Rules for Combining Words

4. By doubling a character referring to a state of a subject (people, objects, etc.), we can also create an accentuated meaning. For example:

大 big ---- 大大 very big
小 small ---- 小小 very small
冷 cold ---- 冷冷 very cold
甜 sweet ---- 甜甜 very sweet

5. By doubling a character referring to an action, we create words with the same meaning. Such words are popular in spoken language and usually go with mild tones. For example:

看 to look ---- 看看 to have a look
想 to think ---- 想想 to think about
试 to try ---- 试试 to have a try
摸 to touch ---- 摸摸 to touch

Note: The following structure is also popularly used:

word for action + 一 + word for action

Examples:

看 to look ---- 看一看 to have a look
想 to think ---- 想一想 to think about
试 to try ---- 试一试 to have a try
摸 to touch ---- 摸一摸 to touch

In addition to these basic cases, some other special structures serve as extensions. Most of these are fixed words and are usually in strong modal colors. For example:

黑乎乎 dark, dusky
亮晶晶 glistening
高高兴兴 happily
蹦蹦跳跳 to scamper about
高高低低 rugged
前前后后 hand and foot; during the whole period

Chapter 4
Advanced Skills in Application

Section 1: The Construction of Complex Words

By repeatedly combining words, we can construct new words that refer to very complicated structures. The following example shows the basic mechanism.

The meaning of the word 车 (vehicle) is vague. It can be combined with other words (see rule TT-3 above) to create new words referring to specific objects:

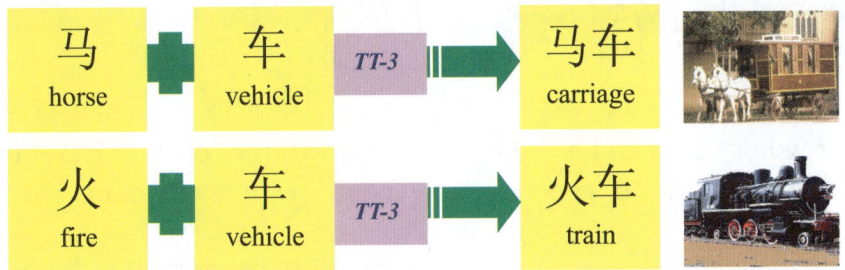

Once a new word is generated by combining other words, the original words interact with each other to produce an entirely new meaning. The point is that each of the original words loses their original meaning in the interaction, and they can only function together in the combination of the new word, as shown in the following chart:

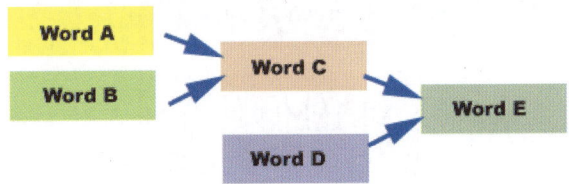

This is similar to what happens when we get water by bonding oxygen and hydrogen. After bonding, the original materials no longer exist; the outcome of their combination (water) is a new object that can be used to do something else. Therefore, even if a word appears to be a complicated combination, it must be regarded as a whole, the same as a word formed by a single character. It can still be combined with other words (whether of single characters or combinations) to make new words with the same principles and rules.

In the examples 马车 (carriage) and 火车 (train), we see that both can be combined with words referring to sizes (for example, 大 and 小) to make new words with more specific meanings.

Chapter 4 Advanced Skills in Application

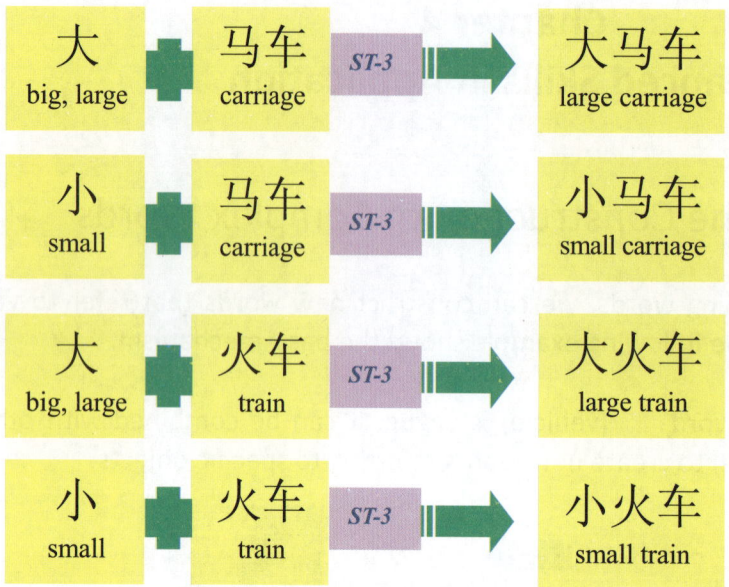

The above four words can then be combined with words for colors (for example, 红色 (red) and 绿色 (green)) to generate new words with even more specific meanings:

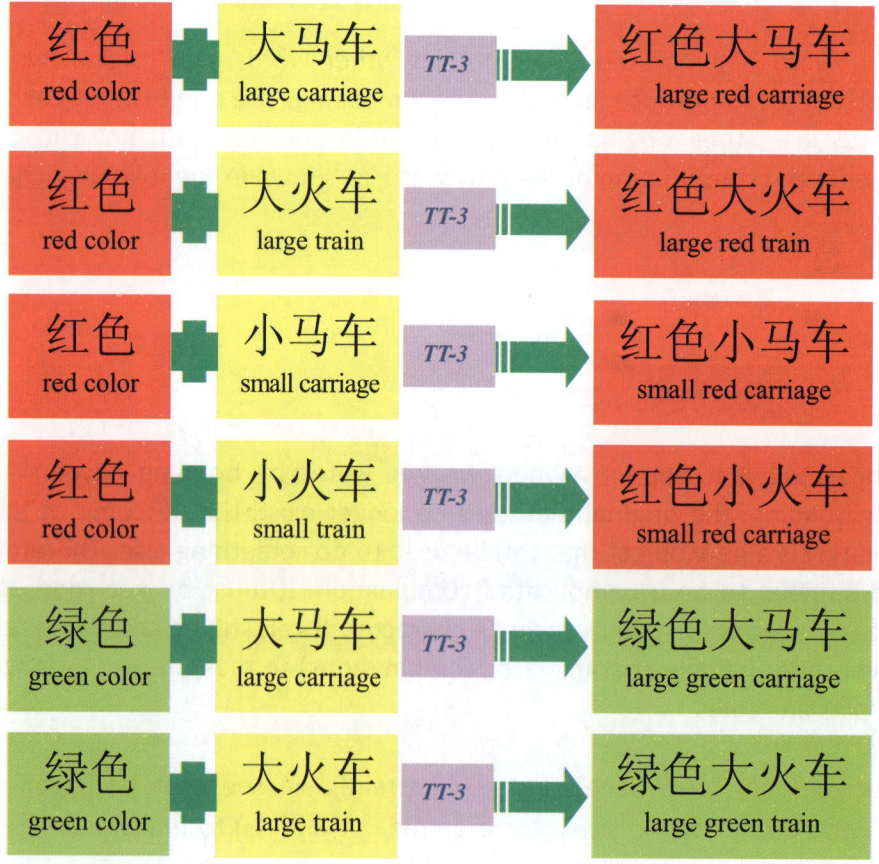

Chapter 4 Advanced Skills in Application

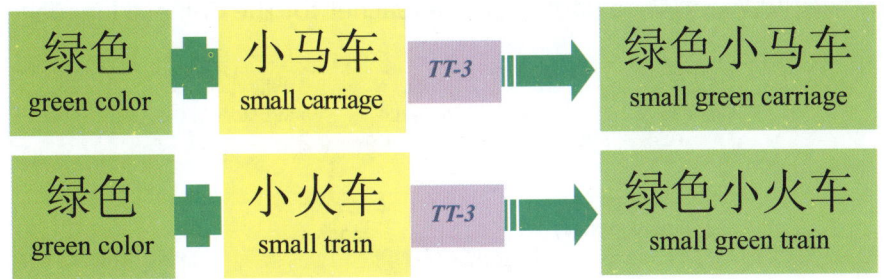

The above examples show the basic method for building words through complicated structures. The following chart illustrates the entire process involved in constructing the word 绿色小火车.

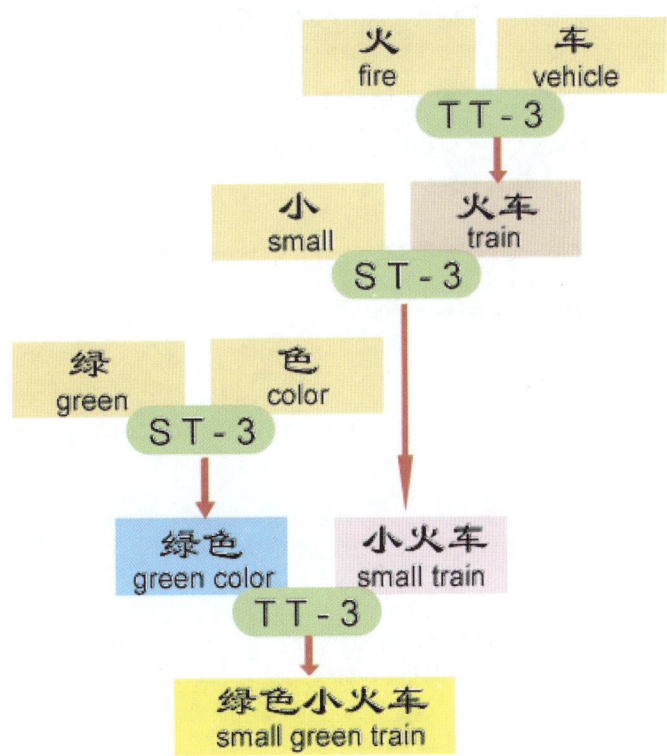

The following examples show further details for applying the principles and rules repetitively to build up a complicated word.

Chapter 4 Advanced Skills in Application

Example 1: 年轻女汉语教师 a young female teacher for the Chinese language

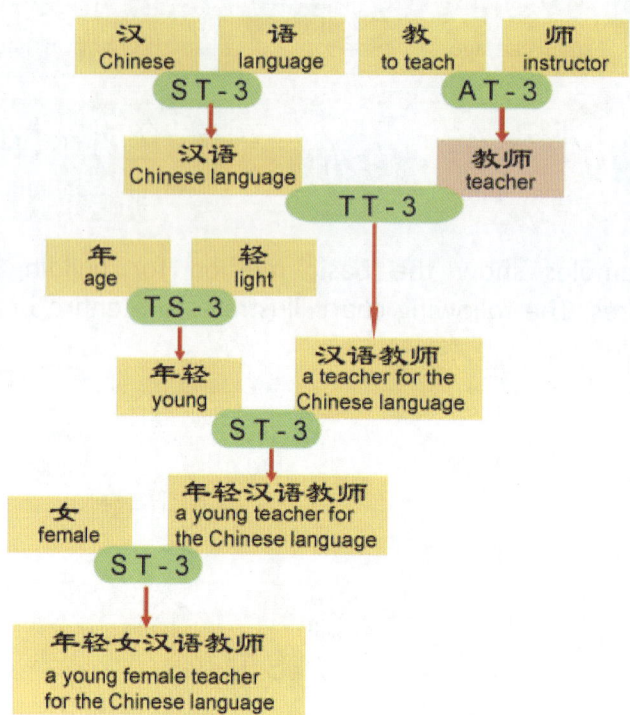

Example 2: 计算机杀毒软件 anti-virus software for computers

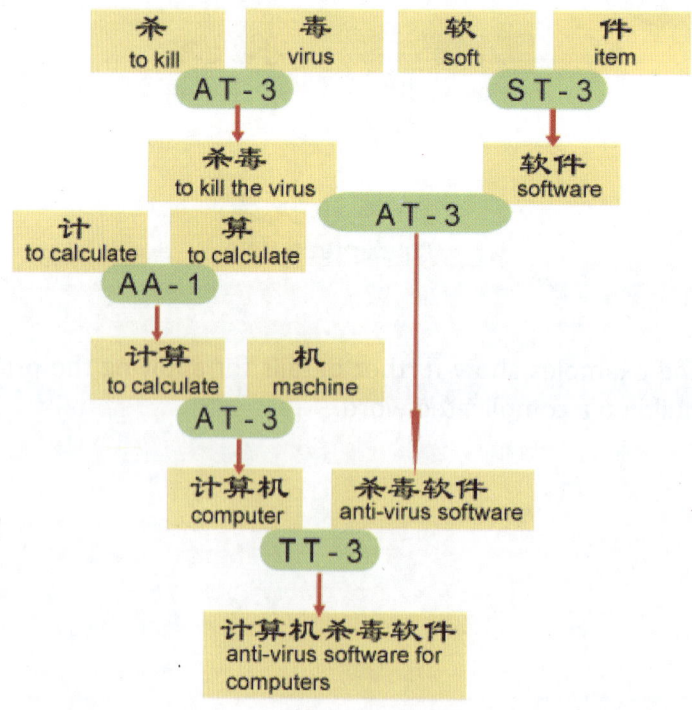

Example 3: 打击侵犯知识产权行为
to punish infringement of intellectual property

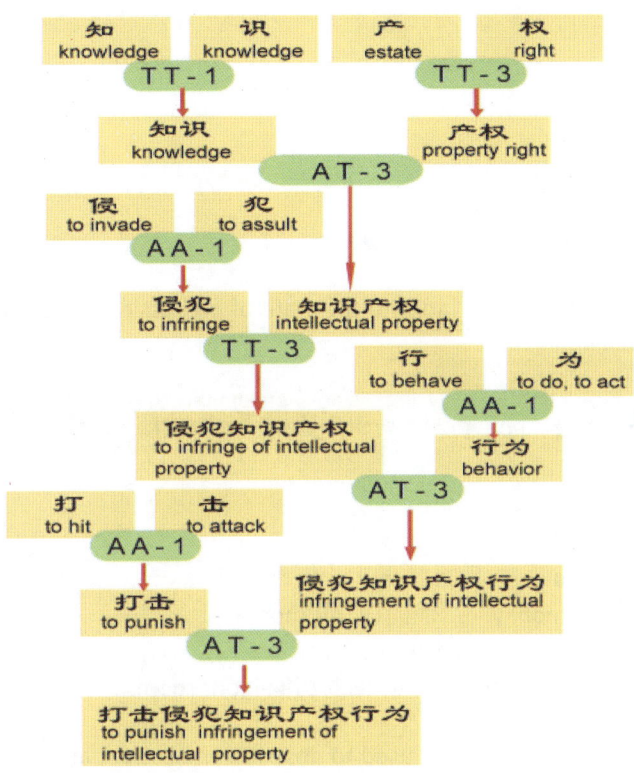

Example 4: 跨国公司财务经理
the financial manager of an international company

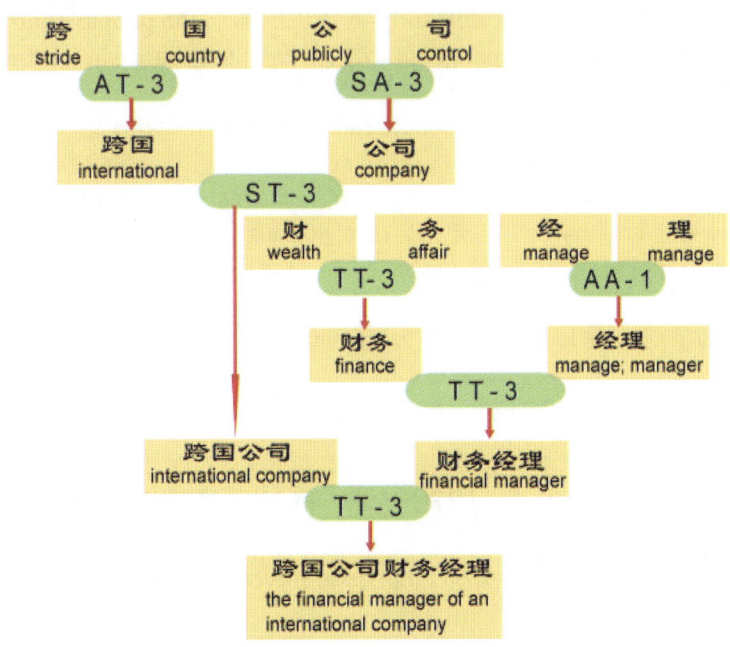

Chapter 4 Advanced Skills in Application

In theory, we can splice tens of characters into a whole for some of the more intricate meanings. However, in everyday language, most words are simple and distinct structures.

 Key Application: Indicating Possession

In the Chinese language, we indicate the state of possessing something by using 的 in a structure, such as:

| the owner | + 的 + | the subject belongs to the owner |

Examples:

我 I + 的 + 书 book ---- 我的书 my book
他 he + 的 + 钱 money ---- 他的钱 his money
你 you + 的 + 车 car ---- 你的车 your car
你们 you + 的 + 房间 room ---- 你们的房间 your rooms

The above structure can also be used to describe an abstract and universal relation. For example:

世界 world + 的 + 和平 peace ---- 世界的和平 the peace of the world
未来 future + 的 + 科技 science ---- 未来的科技 the future of science
人民 the people + 的 + 需求 demand ---- 人民的需求 the people's demand
天气 weather + 的 + 变化 change ---- 天气的变化 the change in weather

In some more literal expressions, people can substitute 的 with 之. For example:

经典 classic + 之 + 作 artwork ---- 经典之作 a classical piece of artwork
光荣 glory + 之 + 战 battle ---- 光荣之战 a glorious fight
大都市 metropolis + 之 + 问题 problem ---- 大都市之问题 the problems of the metropolises
家庭 family + 之 + 爱 love ---- 家庭之爱 family love

The above structure can also be extended as seen below:

| an action | + 的 + | the target or the result of the action |

This structure is popularly used to emphasize the consequence between the action and the subject. For example:

Chapter 4 Advanced Skills in Application

我 I + 想 to think about + 的 + 事 matter, affair ---- 我想的事 the thing I am thinking about

他 he + 关心 to care + 的 + 人 people ---- 他关心的人 the people he cares about

你 you + 走 to walk + 的 + 路 way ---- 你走的路 the way you take

她 she + 写 to write + 的 + 信 letter ---- 她写的信 the letter she writes

A formal way to put the above expressions is:

所 + **an action** + 的 + **the target or the result of the action**

Examples:

我 I + 所 + 想 to think about + 的 + 事 matter, affair ---- 我所想的事 the thing I am thinking about

你 you + 所 + 说 to say + 的 + 话 words ---- 你所说的话 the words you speak

人民 people + 所 + 拥有 to have, to posses + 的 + 力量 ---- 人民所拥有的力量 the power possessed by the people

政府 government + 所 + 发布 to issue + 的 + 政策 policies ---- 政府所发布的政策 the policies issued by the government

Chapter 4 Advanced Skills in Application

 Extra Knowledge: Chinese Idioms

Thousands of Chinese idioms, the priceless treasures of Chinese culture, are widely used in people's daily language, infusing their speeches with both vividness and incisiveness. Most of these idioms come from ancient stories or fairy tales, and you can regard them as either topics or the summarized conclusions of long profound narrations. Just because they appear simple does not mean that they are easy to grasp. For example:

闻鸡起舞

Literal meaning:
To begin drilling once one hears the crows of a cock

Actual meaning:
To make hard and continuous efforts

Background story:
About 1,700 years ago, a tribe from the north of  China was invading the central states of China. Liu Kun and Zu Di, two friends, were very keen to fight the invaders. One day, a cock awakened them in the early morning. Liu Kun was quite angry at the crowing, saying "What an awful noise!" However, Zu Di replied, "No, the cock is reminding us to make strong efforts toward our ideals." They got up and, taking their swords, started practicing. After that, they always began their work soon after cock crowed each day. After several years, they became famous leaders due to their diligence.

狐假虎威

Literal meaning:
A fox relies on a tiger's ferocity

Actual meaning:
To bully people by flaunting one's powerful connections

Background story:
This idiom comes from a fairy tale. A tiger believes 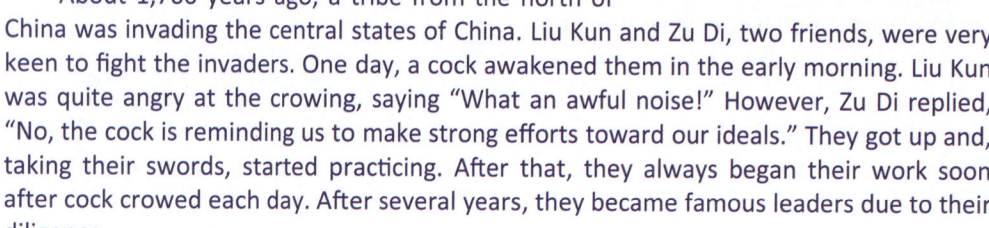 that he is the king of the forest, and other animals, except for a fox, are quite afraid of him because of his sharp teeth and strong claws. The tiger is quite angry at the fox, and one day he catches him. However, the fox threatens the tiger, "I am the real king of this forest, and I am the one all animals are afraid of. If you kill me, every animal will kill you." The tiger does not believe this and orders the fox to prove it. The fox tells the tiger, "Let me ride on your back, then we will walk around together, and you will see the truth." The tiger does so, and indeed, he finds all the other animals rushing away from them. Since that time, the tiger is very careful and respectful around the fox.

Section 2: Principles and Practical Skills

In the previous section, several complex words are mentioned:

年轻女汉语课老师 a young female teacher of the Chinese language
打击侵害知识产权行为 to punish infringement of intellectual property
跨国公司财务经理 the financial manager of an international company

In practical language, a more popular way of saying the above is:

年轻女汉语课老师 ---- 年轻的女汉语课老师
跨国公司财务经理 ---- 跨国公司的财务经理
打击侵犯知识产权行为 ---- 打击侵犯知识产权的行为

In complex words, especially those constructed by three or more combined words, 的 is frequently adopted to mark the internal structure, as shown in the following examples:

Example 1:

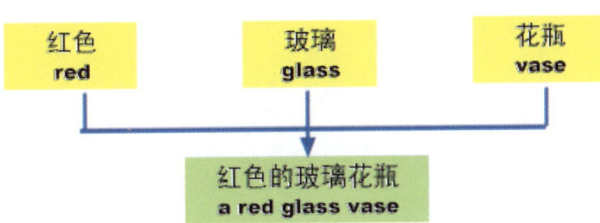

Example 2:

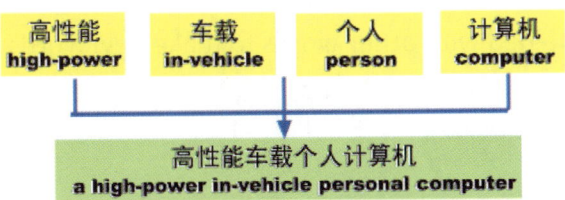

Example 3:

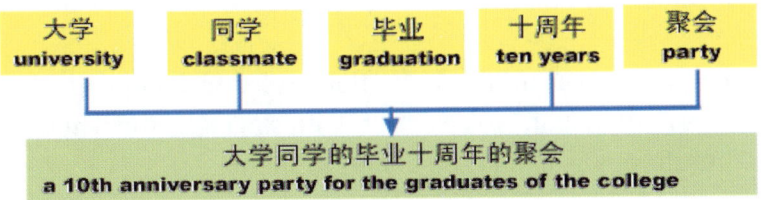

Chapter 4 Advanced Skills in Application

Example 4:

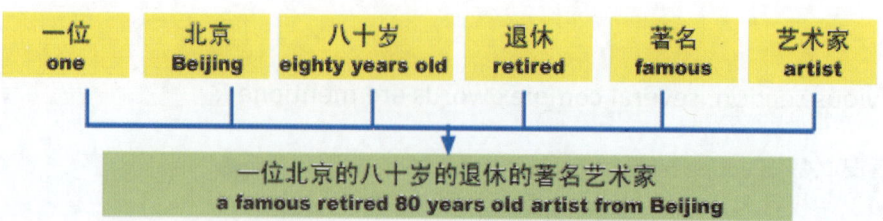

There is a set of principles and rules for applying 的. The following help illustrate these principles and rules.

In Chapter 3 Section 2, we created a new word by combining two characters:

As the word 高音 refers to an independent and unique object, it should be regarded as a basic word. To add 的 to the word will change the meaning. For example:

高音 high-pitched voice
高的音 sound with high frequency

高人 able person
高的人 tall people

小车 car
小的车 small-sized vehicle

The word 高音 can further be combined with other words to make new words:

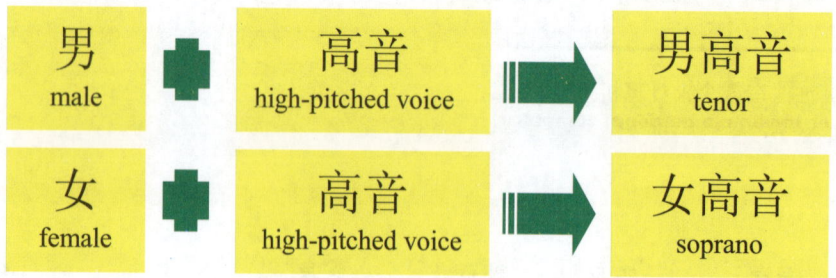

Here, the two new words, 男高音 and 女高音, both refer to independent and unique objects (specific types of human voices found in singing), and should be regarded as basic words. Therefore, 的 cannot be added to them.

Chapter 4 Advanced Skills in Application

The above two words can be combined still further to generate new words with new meanings:

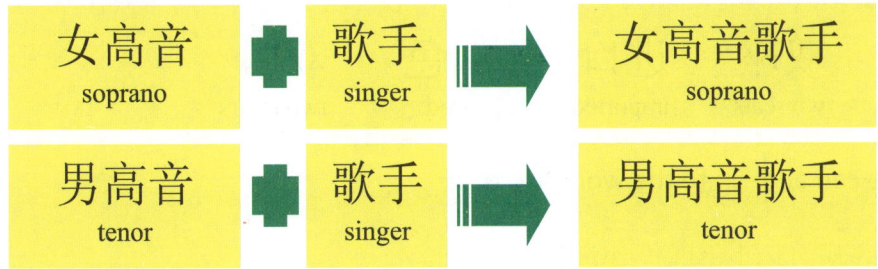

The new words both refer to objects that are independent and unique (specific types of singers), and they should be regarded as basic words even though they are constructed of three combinations. It is neither necessary nor acceptable to add 的 to them.

Suppose that there are two 女高音歌手 (sopranos): one is 有名 (famous) and the other is 无名 (nameless). We can combine 有名 and 无名 with 女高音歌手 respectively to get two new words:

In this case, 有名 and 无名 help specify the various properties of 女高音歌手, and the new words are basic words. They are only temporarily words, and 的 is usually added to make the internal logical structure distinct.

The basic principle is that 的 can never be added into a basic word (no matter how complicated it is). However, even for temporary words, using 的 to indicate the internal structure is an option. That is to say, when a temporary word is easy to understand, it is not necessary to use 的. For example, the following words are also acceptable in practical language:

著名女高音歌手
无名女高音歌手

In practical language, 的 should be applied as infrequently as possible because too many 的 in a word results in wordy or boring language. The following example shows how to use 的 properly.

073

Chapter 4 Advanced Skills in Application

All of the following words can be combined with 小汽车 (car) to make a word to describe a specific car:

 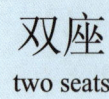   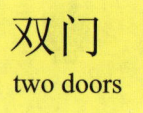

In theory, we can add 的 to the word like this:

高级的进口的双座的双门的红色的小汽车
an imported luxury two-seated two-door red car

In practical language, people never repeat 的 so many times in a word. The more reasonable way to do this is:

高级进口双座双门的红色小汽车

高级的进口的双座双门红色小汽车

高级的进口双座双门的红色的小汽车

高级的进口的双座双门的红色的小汽车

Note: in spoken language, a simpler way of saying complicated words is to pause between them in speaking. For example:

高级 (a halt)　进口(a halt)　双座 (a halt)　双门(a halt)　红色(a halt)　小汽车

The literal form is:

高级、进口、双座、双门、红色、小汽车

Below is a gallery of extensions using 的 in combination to create new words.

Case 1:

As discussed in Chapter 2 Section 1, under rule TT-3, a new word can be created by combining two words that describe the features of a certain object. For example:

In the construction of complicated combinations under TT-3, 的 is frequently used to indicate the internal structure of the words. For example:

Chapter 4 Advanced Skills in Application

晚上 evening + 电影 movie ---- 晚上的电影 the movie in the evening
晚上 evening + 会议 conference ---- 晚上的会议 a conference held in the evening
春天 spring + 衣服 clothes ---- 春天的衣服 the clothes for spring
春天 spring + 花 flower ---- 春天的花 the flowers in spring
中国 China + 发展 development ---- 中国的发展 the development of China

的 is also frequently used in words referring to people with specific features. For example:

六个月 six months + 宝贝 baby ---- 六个月的宝贝 a baby of six months
三十岁 30 years old + 男人 man ---- 三十岁的男人 a man aged 30
初中 middle school + 学生 students ---- 初中(的)学生 students in middle school
航空 aviation + 专家 specialist ---- 航空的专家 a specialist in aviation

Case 2:

As discussed in Chapter 3 Section 2, a new word can be generated under rule ST-3 when a word referring to a state is combined with one referring to an object. For example:

This is a most popular and productive method of creating new words. In the constructing of a complex word in ST-3, 的 is usually applied to indicate the internal structure. For example:

热烈 enthusiastic + 气氛 atmosphere ---- 热烈的气氛 enthusiastic atmosphere
冰冷 ice-cold + 房间 room ---- 冰冷的房间 an ice-cold room
芳香 fragrant + 味道 smell ---- 芳香的味道 a fragrant smell
坚固 firm + 防线 line of defense ---- 坚固的防线 a firm line of defense
温暖 warm + 笑容 smile ---- 温暖的笑容 a warm smile
聪明 wise + 回答 answer ---- 聪明的回答 a wise answer

Case 3:

By combining a word referring to an action with one referring to the consequence of the action, we create a word implying "an object that resulted from a certain action", which falls under rule AT-3. For example:

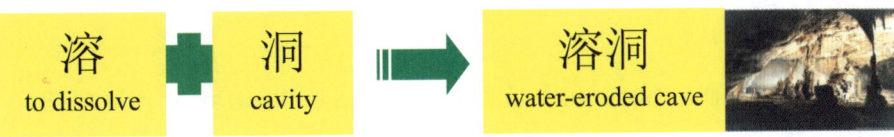

075

Chapter 4 Advanced Skills in Application

This rule can also be extended into more complicated situations, and 的 is frequently used in the complex words constructed. For example:

争论 to argue + 结果 result ---- 争论的结果 the result of the argument
研究 to research, to explore + 结果 result ---- 研究的结果 the result of the research
发布 to release + 消息 news ---- 发布的消息 the news release
工作 to work + 成果 production ---- 工作的成果 the production of work
规划 to plan + 前景 outlook, future ---- 规划的前景 the future planned
撞击 to hit, to impact + 痕迹 mark, trail ----撞击的痕迹 the mark of an impact

> **Comparing:**
>
> 发布消息   to release news
> 发布的消息 the news release

Case 4:

By combining a word referring to an object with another referring to a specific function or usage, we create a new word referring to a tool or an instrument with a specific function. This falls under rule AT-3.

This rule can also be extended to complicated situations, and 的 is also frequently used in the complex words constructed. For example:

吃 to eat + 东西 item, thing ---- 吃的东西 something to eat
治病 to treat a disease + 方法 method ---- 治病(的)方法 the method of treatment
绘画 to paint + 刀 knife ---- 绘画(的)刀 spatula
操作 to operate + 说明 illustration ---- 操作(的)说明 the directions for operation
洗涤 to lave, to clean + 用品 item, article ---- 洗涤(的)用品 the items for the lavatory
消毒 to disinfect + 药品 medicament ---- 消毒(的) 药品 the medication for disinfecting
烹饪 to cook + 器具 apparatus ---- 烹饪(的)器具 kitchenware

In addition to 的, 地 is also frequently used to indicate the internal structure of a complex word in AS-3. The followings cases show how to apply 地 properly in the construction of complex words.

Case 1:

In Chapter 3 Section 6, the following words were used in illustrating rule AS-3.

Chapter 4 Advanced Skills in Application

| 高飞 to fly high | 低飞 to fly low | 快飞 to fly fast | 慢飞 to fly slowly |

This rule can also be extended to complicated situations. Most of the complex words (or phrases) created this way are only for temporary use, and 地 should be added to them to indicate the internal structure. For example, the following words can be used to describe a bird's flight.

| 迅速 rapidly | 缓慢 slowly | 平稳 smoothly | 优雅 elegantly |

When the above words are combined with 飞, add 地 to the complex words. For example:

迅速 rapidly + 地 + 飞 to fly ---- 迅速地飞 to fly rapidly
缓慢 slowly + 地 + 飞 to fly---- 缓慢地飞 to fly slowly
平稳 smoothly + 地 + 飞 to fly---- 平稳地飞 to fly smoothly
优雅 elegantly + 地 + 飞 to fly---- 优雅地飞 to fly elegantly

This mechanism plays an important role in making complex words for the description of specific actions. For example:

轻轻 slightly + 地 + 关门 to close the door ---- 轻轻地关门 to close the door slightly
温柔 tenderly + 地 + 抚摩 to touch ---- 温柔地抚摩 to touch tenderly
彻底 thoroughly + 地 + 清洗 to clean, to wash ---- 彻底地清洗 to clean thoroughly
持续 continuously + 地 + 努力 to make effort ---- 持续地努力 to make a continuous effort
深入 intensively + 地 + 研究 to research ---- 深入地研究 to research intensively
轻松 easily + 地 + 取胜 to win ---- 轻松地取胜 to win easily

Case 2:

Following rule AS-3, we can create a word referring to an action that happens in a specific state, or in a specific trend. For example:

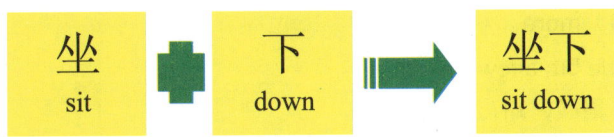

This rule is widely used to create complex words that describe actions. In most cases, 地 should be added to the complex word constructed. For example:

Chapter 4 Advanced Skills in Application

完成 to finish + 地 + 漂亮 nicely ---- 完成地漂亮 to get the work done nicely
掌握 to grasp + 地 + 透彻 thoroughly ---- 掌握地全面 to grasp thoroughly
清洗 to wash + 地 + 干净 clean, neat ---- 清洗地干净 to wash (something) clean
调查 to investigate + 地 + 清楚 thoroughly ---- 调查地清楚 to investigate (something) thoroughly

得 is widely used in constructing complex words for the description of the state of an action. For example:

飞 to fly + 得 + 迅速 rapid ---- 飞得迅速 (to be) rapid in flight
跑 to run + 得 + 很快 very rapid ---- 跑得很快 (to be) very rapid in running
讲 to speak + 得 + 精彩 wonderful ---- 讲得精彩 (to be) wonderful in making a speech
发展 to develop + 得 + 迅速 rapid ---- 发展的迅速 (to be) rapid in developing

得 can also be used to construct a complex word that implies the capability of doing something. For example:

看 to read + 得 + 懂 to understand ---- 看得懂 (to be able to) understand after reading
学 to learn + 得 + 会 capable ---- 学得会 (to be able to) learn
跳 to jump + 得 + 高 high ---- 跳得高 (to be able to) jump high
游 to swim + 得 + 远 far ---- 游得远 (to be able to) swim far

Note: there is currently a strong trend to consolidate 的, 地 and 得 into 的.

 Quick Reference:

Here is a list of the most commonly used words that refer to various extents, degrees and ranges. Refer to a dictionary for details regarding their use.

Degree	很（非常，十分，特别，相当）very
	太 very, too
	最（极，极其）most, extremely
	挺 rather, quite
	特别 especially, extraordinarily
	更（更加）more
	有点 a little bit; a few
	稍（略，稍微，略微）slightly

078

Range	都（总共，总共，全，全部）all 只 only 仅仅 only, merely 一律 all
Frequency	总（总是，从来，一直，一向）always 常（经常、通常、时常、往往）usually, frequently 渐渐（慢慢）gradually 最后（最终，终于）finally 屡次 repeatedly 再（重新）again 偶尔（有时）now and then
Timeliness	突然（猛然）suddenly 迅速（快速，飞速，迅猛）rapidly 缓慢（慢慢）slowly

 Key Application: Special Structures

1. Here is another structure frequently used for the description of an action that proceeds in an orderly manner.

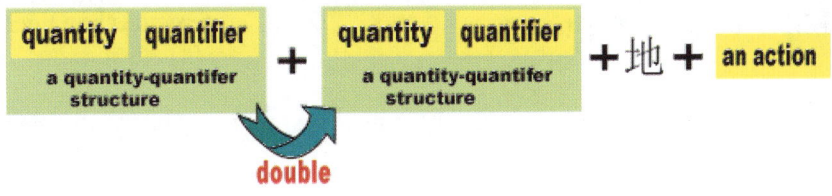

Examples:

一步 one step + 一步 one step + 地 + 走 to walk ---- 一步一步地走 to walk step by step

一口 one bit + 一口 one bit + 地 + 吃 to eat ---- 一口一口地吃 to eat bit by bit

一句 one sentence + 一句 one sentence + 地 + 说 to say ---- 一句一句地说 to speak sentence by sentence

一页 one page + 一页 one page + 地 + 看 to read, to watch ---- 一页一页的看 to read page by page

Based on the above basic structure, other popularly used structures that serve as extensions include the following examples:

一步 one step + 步 (step) + 地 + 走 to walk ---- 一步步地走 ---- to walk step by step

一步 one step + 一个脚印 one footprint + 地 + 前进 ---- 一步一个脚印地前进 to push forward little by little

一点 one drop + 一滴 one drop + 地 + 学习 to learn ---- 一点一滴地学习 to learn bit by bit

三天 three days + 两头 two days + 地 + 出错 to make a mistake ---- 三天两头地出错 to make mistakes frequently

2. The meaning of some words contains a trope:

火红 fiery red

蛙跳 leapfrog

This mechanism can be extended to constructs that are more complicated. A popular structure is to construct the words with 象 and 一样. For example:

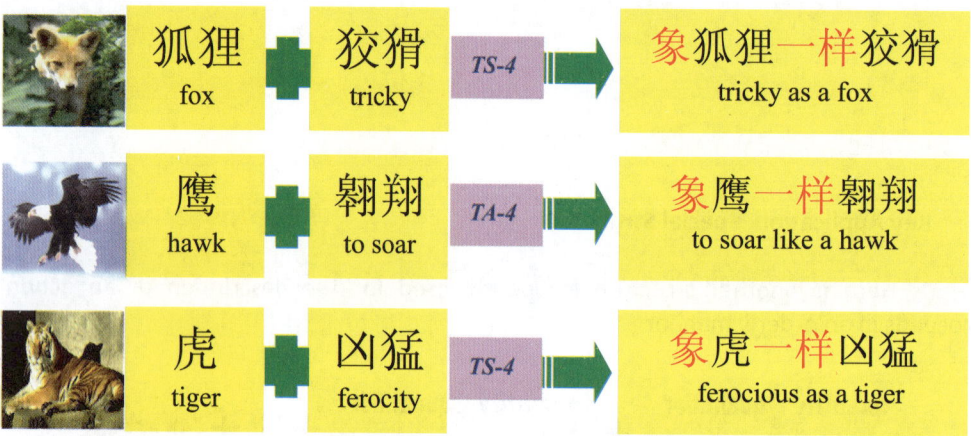

狐狸 fox → 狡猾 tricky → TS-4 → 象狐狸一样狡猾 tricky as a fox

鹰 hawk → 翱翔 to soar → TA-4 → 象鹰一样翱翔 to soar like a hawk

虎 tiger → 凶猛 ferocity → TS-4 → 象虎一样凶猛 ferocious as a tiger

Note: There are other structures used for such expressions. The most common are 如 (如同, 同, 似)...一般 (一样)...

Extra Knowledge: Abbreviations

Although we can combine tens of characters together to express a very complicated meaning, we prefer making things simple and easy for both reading and writing. A common method is to abstract several key characters from a word just as we make abbreviations in English. For example:

高等院校 universities and institutes for higher education ---- 高校
高等教育 higher education ---- 高教
幼儿老师 teachers for kids ---- 幼师
电影评论 review of movies ---- 影评
北京天津塘沽高速公路 the express way from Beijing to Tianjin and Tanggu ---- 京津塘高速

Chapter 5
Sentence Construction

The difference between words and sentences is that words (no matter how complicated they are) only provide isolated and static meanings. Sentences always relate to specific environments and have their specific target for communication no matter how simple they are. A sentence can be made of a simple word, or a complex word, or a group of words specifically structured.

Actually, a sentence, even one in a complicated structure, can also be regarded as an independent word. This is because a sentence can be combined with other words to make new words, or be integrated into another sentence structure to construct new sentences. The following chart illustrates this interesting mechanism.

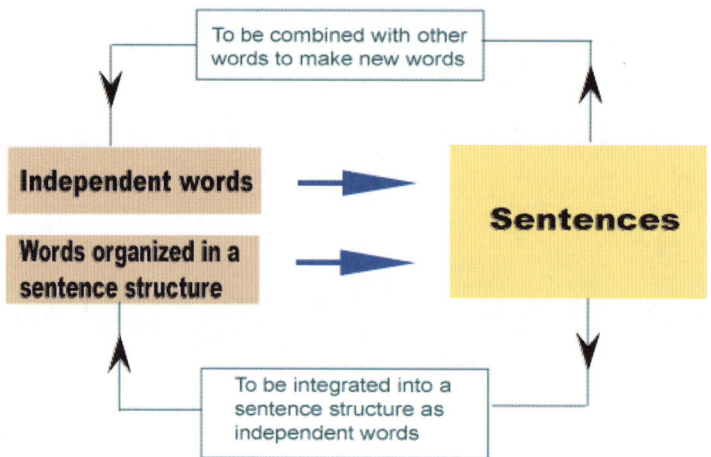

The following examples help illustrate the relations between words and sentences:

我在北京。
I am in Beijing.
Key words: 我 I 在 (be) in 北京 Beijing

Note: The key words in a sentence are listed to aid comprehension. If necessary, the key steps in constructing a sentence are also listed.

The entire sentence can be regard as an independent word referring to a specific state, and then combined with other words to get a new word referring to a more specific meaning. For example, by combining the sentence with 日子 (day) as in ST-3, we can create a complex word:

Chapter 5 Sentence Construction

我在北京 I am in Beijing + 的 + 日子 day ---- 我在北京的日子 the days when I am in Beijing

Here is another example:

他轻松通过了考试。
He passed the exam easily.
Key words: 他 he 轻松 easily 通过 to pass 考试 exam 了 a particle indicates that something happened

This sentence can be combined with 消息 (message) to make a complex word:

他轻松通过了考试 + 的 + 消息 message ---- 他轻松通过了考试的消息 the message that he passed the exam easily

A sentence can also be integrated into the structure of another sentence. For example:

我们知道他轻松通过了考试。
We heard that he passed the exam easily.
Key words: 我们 we 知道 to know

我们知道他轻松通过了考试的消息。
We heard that he passed the exam easily.

Sentence structures in the Chinese language can be classified into several main categories according to their specific functions:

1. To make an order or a suggestion;
2. To describe the action and its influence;
3. To make a comment or a judgment;
4. To describe the occurrence or the existence of a specific subject.

In the following chapters, we will go into detail about the typical structures, along with the rules and skills for creating sentences.

Chapter 5 Sentence Construction

Section 1: Typical structure: Orders and Suggestions

In most cases, there are two essential elements in a sentence making an order or suggestion:

1. One is the subject to whom the order (or suggestion) is given to;
2. The other is a description of the action to be finished.

Therefore, the basic sentence structure is:

subject talked about + **action preferred to be accomplished**
Structure code: OS (Orders and Suggestions) -1

Note: Each sentence structure is given a unique code for quick reference.

OS-1 can be considered an extension of rule TA-3. In TA-3, by combining a word that refers to a subject with one referring to an action issued by the subject, we create a new word referring to a specific action issued by a certain subject. For example:

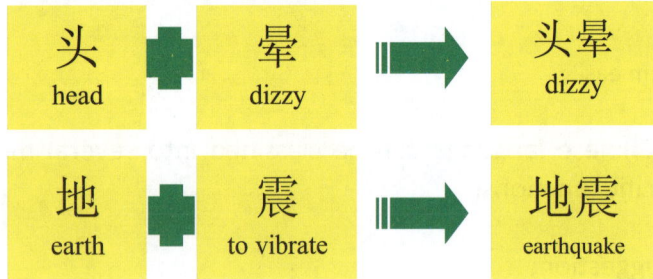

The basic mechanism in TA-3 is also applicable for universal situations. That is to say, each of the essential components in TA-3 can be extended to a complicated form, which appears as either a complex word construction with many characters or a sentence functioning as a word. For example:

您坐！
Sit down please!
Key words: 您 you 坐 to sit

您进来！
Come in please!
Key words: 您 you 进来 to come in

您喝茶！
Have some tea!
Key words: 请 please 喝 to drink 茶 tea

大家安静!
Everybody be quiet!
Key words: 大家 everybody 安静 quiet; to calm down

您向我们发表一下您的看法!
Please tell us your opinion!
Key words: 请 please 您 you 向 to, towards 我们 we, us 发表 to show, to utter 您的 you 看法 viewpoint, opinion 一下 a quantity-quantifier structure
Key steps: 发表一下您的看法 is a complex word constructed by 发表一下 and 你的想法 in rule A T - 3.

In some cases, it is not necessary to specify the subject, and OS-1 can be simplified into a structure like:

Structure code: OS (Orders and Suggestions) -2

For example:

现在去吧!
Go now!
Key words: 现在 now 去 to go

请进来!
Please come in!
Key words: 请 please 进来 to come in

快走!
Hurry up!
Key words: 快 fast 走 to go

轻轻地关门!
Shut the door lightly!
Key words: 轻轻 slightly 关 to close 门 door

待会再说!
We will talk about that later!
Key words: 待会 later 再 once more; again 说 to talk

The following words are frequently used in orders and suggestions to indicate specific tones:

请 please
必须 (务必应该, 应当, 该, 要, 应) should, ought to, must
最好 had better

Chapter 5 Sentence Construction

For example:

请您参观一下!
Please have a visit!
Key words: 请 please 您 you 参观 to visit

你必须准时到那!
You must be there on time!
Key words: 你 you 必须 must 准时 on time 到 to go, to arrive 那 there

你应当(应该,该,应)更谦虚一点!
You should be a little more modest!
Key word: 你 you 应当 should 谦虚 be modest 一点 a bit, a little

你最好马上离开!
You had better leave at once!
Key words: 你 you 最好 had better 马上 at once 离开 to leave

The following words are frequently used to stop someone from doing something:

不准 不许 不得 严禁 禁止 别 不要 勿 切勿 莫 莫要

They should be placed before the words referring to the actions. For example:

禁止拍照!
No camera!
Key words: 拍照 to take photos

不许进入!
No entrance!
Key words: 进入 to enter, to get in

不准离开这里!
Do not leave (Stay)!
Key words: 离开 to leave 这里 here

你别相信他的谎言!
Do not believe his lies.
Key words: 你 you 相信 to believe 他的 his 谎言 lies

Based on the structure of OS-1 and OS-2, we can create sentences in complicated forms. For example:

你就在这里等他!
You wait for him right here!

Key words: 你 you 就 just, merely 在 at 这里 here 等 to wait 他 him

你们必须今天做完这个工作！
You must finish this work today!
Key words: 你们 you (pl) 必须 must 今天 today 做完 to finish, to complete 工作 job, work

请您十分钟后在门口等我！
Please wait for me at the gate in ten minutes.
Key words: 请 please 您 you 十分钟 ten minutes 后 after 在 at 门口 gate 等 to wait

The quantity-quantifier structure for actions is also popularly used in creating other such sentences. For example:

请你认真地检查一下。
Please check (it) carefully.
请 please 你 you 认真 carefully 检查一下 to check around

你要好好试几次！
You should try it seriously several times.
你 you 要 should 好好 seriously 试 to try 几次 several times

请一步一步地做这个工作。
Please do this job systematically.
请 please 一步一步 step by step 做 to do 这个 this 工作 job

你最好一个字一个字地写清楚！
You had better write down the words one by one.
Key words: 你 you 最好 had better 一个字 one word 写 to write 清楚 clearly

请认真考虑考虑！
Please think about it carefully!
Key words: 请 please 认真 carefully 考虑 to think

你仔细检查检查！
You check it carefully!
Key words: 你 you 仔细 carefully 检查 to check, to inspect

你们要好好打扫打扫房间！
You should clean the room thoroughly.
Key words: 你们 you 要 should 好好 carefully 打扫 to clean 房间 room

你最好勇敢尝试尝试！
You had better try it bravely!
Key words: 你 you 最好 had better 勇敢 bravely 尝试 to try

Chapter 5 Sentence Construction

When a subject is required to accomplish a series of independent actions, the words for actions should be arranged according to their logical sequence. The following examples illustrate the method.

Suppose that we ask somebody to come eat an apple, we can have two independent orders:

请到这来！
Please come here!
Key words: 请 please 到 to come 这 here 来 to come

请吃苹果！
Please have an apple!
Key words: 请 please 吃 to eat 苹果 apple

The above two sentences can be integrated into a whole:

请到这来吃苹果！
Please come here to have an apple!

Note: we can regard 到这来吃苹果 as a complex word constructed by two words for various actions according to rule AA-3.

This mechanism is also applicable in universal cases.

More examples:

请到这边交款！
Please come here and make the payment.
Key words: 请 please 来 to come 这边 here; this side 交款 to pay

请按顺序排队上车！
Please stand in line to get on the bus!
Key words: 请 please 按 with; according to 顺序 sequence 排队 queue 上车 to get on board

马上来办公室取文件！
Come to the office to take the files at once!
Key words: 请 please 马上 at once 来 to come 办公室 office 取 to take 文件 file

请你们排好队跟着我坐电梯进入展厅。
Please stand line up and follow me to the elevator to the exhibition hall.
Key words: 排好队 to queue up 跟着我 to follow me 电梯 elevator 展厅 exhibition hall

Chapter 5 Sentence Construction

In some cases, an action influences two different kinds of subjects. Suppose that we have two orders:

请你告诉我。
Please tell me.
Key words: 请 please 你 you 告诉 to tell 我 I, me

请你告诉真相。
Please tell the truth.
Key words: 请 please 你 you 告诉 to tell 真相 truth

There are two subjects related to 告诉 (to tell): One is 我 (me), and the other is 真相 (the truth). We can integrate them into one sentence:

请你告诉我真相。
Please tell me the truth.

Note: in most cases, the word for human being is placed before the word for an object. We rarely say: 请你告诉真相我。

More examples:

请大家给我一个机会！
Please give me a chance!
Key words: 请 please 大家 all, everybody 看 to watch 我 I, me 表演 to show, to perform

请你向我们解释清楚。
Please explain this to us clearly.
Key words: 请 please 向 to 解释 to explain 清楚 clearly

请耐心听他说。
Please listen to his explanation patiently.
Key words: 请 please 耐心 patiently 听 to listen 他 he, him 解释 to explain

我们不能再给对手任何机会！
Do not give any chance to our opponents!
Key words: 我们 we 不能 not to 再 once more; again 对手 opponent 任何 any 机会 chance

089

Chapter 5 Sentence Construction

 Key Application: The Position of a Word for Time or Location in a Sentence

If a certain action is closely related in time or location, we should combine the words for time (or location) with the words for the action into a complex word. The most commonly used structure is:

在(于) + **word for time** + 在(于) + **word for location** + **word for an action**

Examples:

在早上六点起床	get up at six in the morning
于三月二十日出发	leave on 20th, March
在北京工作	work in Beijing
(在) 去年在中国学习	studied in China last year

Note: Sometimes people omit 在 before the word for time. In addition to 在 and 于, there are other words frequently used for specifying various features of a time or a location.

> **Comparing:**
>
> 明天叫你的朋友来!
> **Tomorrow, please invite your friends to come here.**
>
> 请你的朋友明天来!
> **Please invite your friends to come here tomorrow.**

Extra Knowledge: Multi-meanings of a Sentence

It is quite common for some characters to have several different core meanings. Example:

热
1. heat, energy in physics that can cause a rise in temperature
2. hot, antonym of cold
3. to heat up, to warm up
4. ardent, warmhearted
5. envious, eager
6. popular; in great demand.

Thus, it is possible for a combination using these characters to have diverse meanings. For example:

热水
1. warm water, hot water   (combined in ST-3)
2. to heat water; to warm water up   (combined in AT-3)

Such phenomena also appear in sentences. For example:

我需要热水。
Possible meaning 1:   I need hot water.
Possible meaning 2:   I need to heat the water.

很多国家需要进口食品。
Possible meaning 1:   Many countries need imported food.
Possible meaning 2:   Many countries need to import food.

Chapter 5 Sentence Construction

Section 2: Typical Structure: Describing the Actions

To describe a subject that performs an action, we can use the following sentence structure:

subject that performs an action + action
Structure code: DA ((Describe an Action)) -1

Note: DA-1 can also be regarded as an extension of rule TA-3, in which we create words 地震 and 头晕. OS-1 is also an extension of the same rule. We can also make orders and suggestions using DA-1.

Examples:

她在哭。
She is crying.
Key words: 她 she, her 哭 to cry

我明天到。
I will arrive tomorrow.
Key words: 明天 tomorrow 到 to arrive

雨一直在下。
It is raining all the time.
Key words: 雨 rain 一直 always 下 to fall
Note: Here, 在 denotes that something is happening now.

科学技术在不断进步。
Scientific technology keeps improving.
Key words: 科学 science 技术 technology 不断 continuously 进步 to develop, to improve

To describe the fact that a subject issues a certain action and directly influences another subject, we can use the following sentence structure:

subject that performs an action + action + subject influenced
Structure code: DA (Describe an Action) -2

Examples:

我喜欢音乐。
I love music.
Key words: 我 I, me 喜欢 to love, to like 音乐 music

他在玩计算机游戏。
He is playing the computer game.
Key words: 他 he, him 玩 to play 计算机 computer 游戏 game

工人们在修理汽车。
The workers are repairing the car.
Key words: 工人们 workers 修理 to repair 汽车 car

孩子们经常去公园。
The kids often go to the park.
孩子们 kids 经常 often, usually 去 to go 公园 park

DA-2 can be regarded as composite of TA-3 and AT-3. In the above sentence structure, the final two parts can also be seen as a description for an action. The following chart shows the internal structure of DA-2:

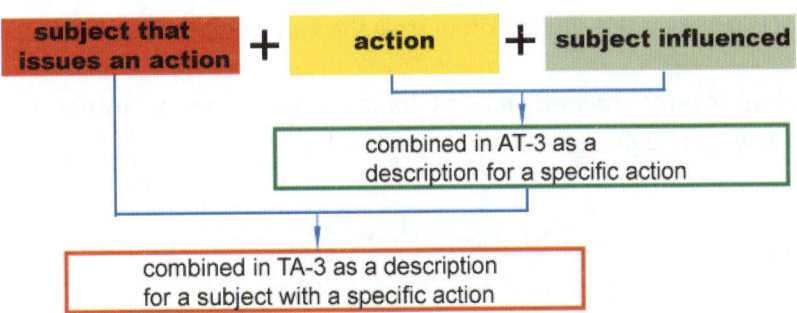

As there is no distinct boundary separating basic words and complex words, in the sentence 他在做饭, the word 做饭 can be regarded as either a basic word or a complex word. Thus, this sentence can be coded several ways:

他在做 饭。

他在做 饭。

Each component in the sentence structure can be extended into a complicated form. The following examples show how to do it systematically.

猫偷走了香肠。
The cat stole the sausages.
Key words: 猫 cat 偷走 to filch, to steal 香肠 sausage

他的猫偷走了香肠。
His cat stole the sausages.

他的花猫偷走了香肠。
His spotted cat stole the sausages.

Chapter 5 Sentence Construction

他的小花猫偷走了香肠。
His spotted kitten stole the sausages.

他的小花猫偷走了我的香肠。
His spotted kitten stole my sausages.

他的小花猫偷走了我做的香肠。
His spotted kitten stole the sausages I made.

他的小花猫偷走了我昨天做的香肠。
His spotted kitten stole the sausages I made yesterday.

今天上午他的小花猫偷走了我昨天做的香肠。
This morning his spotted kitten stole the sausages I made yesterday.

今天上午他的小花猫在我家偷走了我昨天做的香肠。
This morning in my home, his spotted kitten stole the sausages I made yesterday.

When several interconnected actions happen, they can be integrated into one construct with a certain logic sequence. For example:

他开车。
He drove a car.

他去了书店。
(then) He went to the bookstore.

他买了书。
(then) He bought some books.

他开车去书店买了书。
He drove to the bookstore and bought some books.

Other examples:

他去北京开会。
He went to Beijing to have a meeting.
Key words: 他 he 去 to go 北京 Beijing 开会 to have a meeting.

她来北京旅游。
She comes to Beijing for a tour.
Key words: 来 to come 旅游 tour

一只小猫爬到树上去抓鸟。
A kitten climbed up the tree to catch a bird.
Key words: 一只小猫 one kitten 爬 to climb 树 tree 上 up 去 to, for 抓 to catch 鸟 bird

我们明天去博物馆参观展览。

Tomorrow we will go to the museum to see the exhibition.
Key words: 明天 tomorrow 去 to go 博物馆 museum 参观 to visit, to tour 展览 exhibition

As noted at the beginning of this chapter, a sentence can be regarded as an independent word and integrated as such into another sentence. This principle makes it easy to construct a sentence for some very complicated meanings. For example:

他在网上买了几本书。
He bought several books online.
Key words: 网上 online 买 to buy 几本书 several books

他在网上买了几本书花了五十多块钱。
He spent more than 50 bucks to buy some books online.
Key words: 花 to spend 块 buck 钱 money

越来越多的人涌进大城市谋生。
More and more people crowd into large cities to make their living.
Key words: 越来越多 more and more 人 people 涌进 to swarm into 大城市 mega polis 谋生 to make one's living

越来越多的人涌进大城市谋生带来了很多问题。
Many problems arise as more and more people crowd into large cities to make their living.
Key words: 带来 to bring 很多 many, a lot of 问题 question, problem

他的猫偷走了我的香肠。
His cat stole my sausages.
Key words: 猫 cat 偷走 to steal, to filch

邻居看到他的猫偷走了我的香肠。
The neighbor saw his cat steal my sausages.
Key words: 邻居 neighbor 看到 to see, to find

你的汉语说得很好。
You speak Chinese very well.
Key words: 汉语 Chinese 说 to speak, to talk 很好 very well; very good

我们都很羡慕你的汉语说得很好。
We are all envious that you speak Chinese so well.
Key words: 都 all; totally 羡慕 to be envious of

To express negative meanings, 不 or 没 is added directly before the word that refers to the action. For example:

周日我们不工作。
We do not work on Sunday.
Key words: 周日 Sunday 我们 we, us 不 not, no 工作 to work

Chapter 5 Sentence Construction

我现在不想买这件上衣。
I do not want to buy this coat now.
Key words: 我 I, me 现在 now 不 no, not 买 to buy 这件上衣 this coat

昨天他没来看我。
He did not come to see me yesterday.
Key words: 昨天 yesterday 他 he, him 没 no, not 来 to come 看 to see 我 me

你们肯定不知道他很喜欢那个女孩。
You surely do not know that he likes that girl very much.
Key words: 肯定 surely 知道 to know 他 he, him 很 very 喜欢 to like 那个女孩 that girl
Key step: 他很喜欢那个女孩 He likes the girl very much.

Comparing

不 implies that somebody would not do something, and 没 is primarily used for describing a fact. For example:

他不吃饭。	他没吃饭。
He would not eat anything.	**He has not had anything.**
我不告诉你真相。	我没告诉你真相。
I will not tell you the truth.	**I did not tell you the truth.**

Chapter 5 Sentence Construction

 Quick Reference

As we know, some words refer to abstract actions, such as 想 (to think), 希望 (to hope), 能 (can), etc. These words can also be used in this structure. Below are the most commonly used examples (you can find details about them in a dictionary).

想(要, 想要) to want　　希望 to hope　　觉得(认为) to think
决定 to decide　　　　感觉 to feel　　相信 to believe

Examples:

我想(要, 想要)休息一会。
I want to rest for a while.
Key words: 我 I, me　想 to want, to hope, to wish　休息一会 to rest for a while

我觉得（认为）这是个好消息。
I think that this is good news.
Key words: 我 I, me　觉得 to think, to feel　这 this　是 be　好消息 good news
Key step: 这是个好消息 This is good news.

他决定立刻回家。
He decided to go home at once.
Key words: 他 he, him　决定 to decide　立刻 at once　回家 to go home

她相信自己一定会成功。
She believes that she will surely succeed.
Key step: 相信 to believe　自己 oneself　一定 certainly, surely　成功 to succeed

Chapter 5 Sentence Construction

 Key Application: Expressions for Time

Below is a group of words that are commonly used in structuring references to time. They can be considered special quantifiers.

世纪 century　年 year　　　月 month　　周 week　　　天 day
日 day　　　小时 hour　　分 minute　　秒 second　　点 o'clock
时 o'clock　季度 quarter (of year)　　刻 quarter (of an hour)

To express a specific year, date or o'clock, we can add the numbers directly before the corresponding word. For example:

二十一世纪　　　　　　　21st century
一九七五年三月八日　　　March 8th, 1975
十月二十四日五点十五分　5: 15, October 24th
六点零八分五十秒　　　　06:08:50

The following words are frequently combined with the words above to make complex words for various times (mostly in rules ST-3 and TT-3).

今 this　　　明 next　　　后 the one after next　　上（去）last
下 next　　　半 half of　　初 beginning　　　　　　末 end
中 middle　　终 end　　　 本 this

Examples:

今天　　　　明天　　　　　　上月　　　　　　　月初
today　　　tomorrow　　　　last month　　　　beginning of a month
今年　　　　后年　　　　　　上半年　　　　　　年中
this year　the year after next　first half of a year　middle of a year

The following are the words for the days in a week:

Monday	Tuesday	Wednesday	Thursday	Friday	Saturday	Sunday
星期一	星期二	星期三	星期四	星期五	星期六	星期天（日）
周一	周二	周三	周四	周五	周六	周日
礼拜一	礼拜二	礼拜三	礼拜四	礼拜五	礼拜六	礼拜天（日）

Note: Especially in the rural area, people often use the lunar calendar in their daily lives. All Chinese traditional festivals are based on the lunar calendar.

Chapter 5 Sentence Construction

Section 3: Typical Structure: Describing the Subject

There are two basic elements of meaning in sentences for a description or a comment:

1. The subject talked about;
2. The description or the comment.

Sometimes it is not possible to specify the subject, so the simplest sentence structure is:

description or comment
Structure code: DC (Description and Comment) -1

When it is necessary to specify the subject, the structure is:

subject talked about + **description or comment**
Structure code: DC (Description and Comment) -2

Examples:

不错。
Right.

太糟了。
So bad.

真牛。
Unbelievable.

太酷了。
So cool.

他很好。
He is good.
Key words: 他 he 很 very 好 good; well

天气非常好。
The weather is wonderful.
Key words: 天气 weather 非常 very 好 good; well

她的脸很漂亮。
Her face is beautiful.

Chapter 5 Sentence Construction

Key words: 她的 her 脸 face 很 very 漂亮 pretty, beautiful

今天天气有点冷。
The weather is a little bit cold today.
Key words: 今天 today 天气 weather 有点 a bit, a little 冷 cold

这道菜很好吃。
This dish is delicious.
Key words: 这 this 道 quantifier for dishes 好吃 delicious

你的想法真古怪。
Your idea is so weird.
Key words: 你的 your 想法 idea, thought 真 really, so 古怪 weird, eccentric

This structure can be regarded as an extension of rule TS-3, in which we create the word as follows:

The key difference between DC-1 and DA (1, 2) lies in the fact that, in DC-1, the subject does not perform any action.

Each component in this structure can also be extended into a complicated form. For example:

这只白色的小狗真可爱！
This white puppy is really lovely!
Key words: 这只 this 白色 white color 小狗 puppy 真 really, very 可爱 lovely

你做的事非常对。
You did the right thing.
Key words: 你 you 做 do 事 thing, matter 非常 very 对 right, correct
Key step: 做的事 the thing (somebody) does

这辆进口的红色小汽车非常漂亮时尚。
This imported red car is very nice and stylish.
Key words: 辆 quantifier for vehicles 进口 import 红色 red color 漂亮 nice 时尚 vogue, style
Key step: 进口的红色小汽车 an imported red car

他现在面临的任务光荣而艰巨。
The mission he is on is both glorious and tough.
Key words: 现在 now 面临 face 任务 mission 光荣 glory, glorious 艰巨 hard, tough
Key step: 面临的任务 the mission that (somebody) is facing

这几年中国的经济发展得很迅速。
China's economic development is very rapid in recent years.
Key words: 这 this 几 several 经济 economy 发展 development 很 very 迅速 rapid; rapidly
Key step: 这几年 recent years 发展得很迅速 (to be) rapid in developing

We can also make a comment on an incident that is described in another sentence. Examples:

他经常半夜去公园散步。
He usually goes to the park at midnight to take a walk.
Key words: 经常 usually 半夜 midnight 公园 park 散步 to take a walk; to promenade

他经常半夜去公园散步很奇怪。
It is strange that he usually goes to the park to take a walk at midnight.
Key words: 奇怪 strange, weird

他喝了很多酒还要开车回家。
He still wants to drive home after drinking too much.
Key words: 喝 drink 很多 many, much 酒 wine, alcohol 开车 to drive 回家 to go home

他喝了很多酒还要开车回家很危险。
It is dangerous that he still wants to drive home after drinking too much.
Key words: 危险 dangerous

我要在一个小时内完成这个工作。
I should finish this work within one hour.
Key words: 一个小时 one hour 内 in, within 完成 to finish, to accomplish 工作 work, job

我要在一个小时内完成这个工作几乎不可能。
It is almost impossible for me to finish this work within one hour.
Key words: 几乎 almost 不可能 impossible

是 (be) is frequently used in making an introduction, a judgment or a description. The typical sentence structure with 是 is:

subject +是+ **description or comment**
Structure code: DC (Description and Comment) -3

Note: 为 and 乃 are also commonly used in this structure, bringing a more literary tone.

Examples:

我是一个中文老师。
I am a teacher of the Chinese language.
Key words: 我 I, me 是 to be 一个 one 中文 Chinese language 老师 teacher

Chapter 5 Sentence Construction

他身边的女士是他的妻子。
The woman beside him is his wife.
Key words: 他 he, him 身边 aside, beside (somebody) 女士 lady 是 to be 他的 his 妻子 wife

明天要来参观我们学校的客人是一位著名的教授。
The guest that comes to visit our school tomorrow is a famous professor.
Key words: 要 will 参观 to visit 客人 guest 是 to be 著名 famous 教授 professor

这场音乐会的最后一个节目是男高音独唱。
The last piece of this concert is a solo by a tenor.
Key words: 场 quantifier for games, shows, etc. 音乐会 concert 最后 final, last 一个 one 节目 repertoire, piece 是 to be 独唱 solo

In most cases, we should avoid repeating the word for the subject in the latter part of DC-3. The typical sentence structure is:

subject +是+ **description or comment** +的
Structure code: DC (Description and Comment) -4

The following example shows the basic mechanism for omitting such repetition:

这本书是我的书。
This book is mine.
Key words: 这 this 本 quantifier for books 是 to be 我的 my 书 book

There are two 书 in the sentence, and they both refer to the same subject. Thus, we can omit the second one in order to make the sentence more compact without causing any misunderstanding. Therefore, a better sentence is:

这本书是我的。

Other examples:

我的判断是正确的(判断)。
My judgment is correct.
Key words: 判断 to judge; judgment 正确 correct

这辆车是中国生产的(车)。
This vehicle is (a vehicle) made in China.
Key words: 这 this 辆 quantifier for vehicles 车 vehicle 中国 China 生产 to produce, to make

他提的方案是可行的(方案)。
The plan he proposed is (a) feasible (plan).
Key words: 他 he, him 提 to rise, to propose 方案 plan 是 to be 可行 feasible

Chapter 5 Sentence Construction

你们的演出是很成功的(演出)。
Your performance is (a) successful (performance).
Key words: 你们 you (pl) 演出 performance 是 to be 很 very 成功 successful

To express a negative meaning, we usually add 不 before the word for the key words in the description or the comment. For example:

Note: 并非 is also a popular word and is used especially with a formal tone.

他的脾气不好。
His temper is not good.
Key words: 他 he, him 脾气 temper 不 no, not 好 good

让他单独做这项工作不合适。
It is not right to let him finish this job alone.
Key words: 让 to let 单独 alone 做 to do 项 quantifier for works 合适 appropriate

这件事绝对不是他干的。
He did not do this.
Key words: 这 this 件 quantifier for affairs 绝对 definitely 不 no, not 是 to be 干 to do

昨天我买的茶叶并非我的家乡出产的。
The tea I bought yesterday is not produced in my hometown.
Key words: 买 to buy 茶叶 tea 是 to be 家乡 hometown 出产 to make, to produce

 Quick Reference:

Here is a list of the most commonly used structures for describing various time features.

1. 在 + time   at, on, in

在五月五日六点 at 6 o'clock on the 5th of May
在下个月 in next month
在二零零八年 in the year 2008

2. 在（当）+ time (affair) + 的时候（or other words referring to times） when..., at the time of...

当我回家的时候 when I got back home
在他工作的时间 at the time he is working
在鸟迁徙的季节 in the season when the wild geese migrate
当火车开动的时候 when the train moves

Chapter 5 Sentence Construction

3. 在（当）+ time (affair) + 以前（之前）before the time of...

在我毕业以前 before I graduate
在下个周六之前 before next Saturday
在父母回家之前 before parents get back home
在二零零八年之前 before the year 2008

4. 在（当）+ time (affair) + 后（之后，以后）after the time of...

当我结婚以后 after I am married
在九月后 after September
在冬天之后 after the winter
当他开始工作之后 after he starts his job

4. 从（打，自，自从）+ time (affair) + 起（开始） since, from

从你开始学习汉语起 since you started learning the Chinese language
自去年八月开始 since last August
自从我们认识开始 since we knew each other
打明天起 from tomorrow

5. 到 （直到，一直到，至）+ time (affair) + 为止 till, until

到刚才为止 until now
到明年一月为止 until next January
到你明白了为止 until you understand that
到雨停了为止 until the rain stops

6. 从（打，自，自从）+ time (affair) + 到（直到，一直到，至）+ time (affair) + 为止 (not always necessary) from...to...

从星期一到星期五 from Monday to Friday
打明天到下个周日 from tomorrow to next Sunday
自从他们来到中国直到他们离开 from the time that they arrived in China until they left
打春节前一直到元宵节 from the Spring Festival to the Lantern Festival

Chapter 5 Sentence Construction

 Extra Knowledge: Expressing Exclamation

To express exclamation in the Chinese language, one simply needs to add words indicating strong emotion into a sentence. The most commonly used words are 多, 多么, 真, 太 and 特别. The following examples show the basic mechanism in expressing exclamations:

今天天气好。
The weather is very good today.
Key words: 今天 today 天气 weather 好 good; well

We can add 太 and 啦 into the above sentence to make an exclamation.

今天天气太好啦！
What a good weather today!

Other examples:

他是一个多么聪明的孩子！
What a smart child he is!
Key words: 他 he, him 一个 one 聪明 smart 孩子 child, kid

这条小溪太清了！
How clear this brook is!
Key words: 这条小溪 this brook 清 clear

你买的这件衣服真贵啊！
What an expensive coat you bought!
Key words: 你 you 买 buy 这件衣服 this clothes 贵 expensive

In fact, there are other ways to show exclamation, for example, a stressed tone or an exaggerated gesture can also express strong emotion.

Chapter 5 Sentence Construction

Section 4: Typical Structure: Describing Existence

The most popular sentence structure for describing the existence or the occurrence of a subject is:

time + location + 有 + subject
Structure code: DE (Description of the Existence) -1

Note: The components for time and location are not always essential.

Examples:

在湖里有条船。
There is a boat on the lake.
Key word: 在 at, in, on 湖 lake 里 inside 条 quantifier for ships 船 ship

刚才在房间里有很多人。
There were many people in this room just now.
Key words: 刚才 just now 在 at, in, on 房间里 in the room 很多人 many people

以前这个村子外有条小河。
There was a brook outside this village before.
Key words: 以前 before 这个村子 this village 外 outer 条 quantifier for rivers 小河 brook

很久以前这个森林里有很多种野兽。
A long time ago, there were many kinds of animals in this forest.
Key words: 久 long 以前 before 森林 forest 里 inside 很多 many 种 kind, type 野兽 beast
Key step: 很久以前 a long time ago 很多种 many kinds of

下个月这个剧院会有精彩的歌剧。
There will be a wonderful opera in this opera house.
key words: 下 next 个 a quantifier 这 this 剧院 opera house 精彩 wonderful 歌剧 opera

在我的计算机里有很多重要的文件。
There are many important files in my computer.
Key words: 在 at, in, on 计算机 computer 里 inside 很多 many 重要 important 文件 file

Each component of this structure can also be extended to a complicated form, as shown by the following examples:

在博物馆有展览。
There is an exhibition in the museum.
Key words: 在 at, in, on 博物馆 museum 展览 exhibition

Chapter 5 Sentence Construction

今天在博物馆有展览。
There is an exhibition in the museum today.

今天在天安门附近的博物馆有展览。
There is an exhibition in the museum near Tian'anmen Square today.

今天在天安门附近的博物馆有文物展览。
There is an exhibition of cultural relics in the museum near Tian'anmen Square today.

今天在天安门附近的博物馆有中国古代文物展览。
There is an exhibition of ancient Chinese cultural relics in the museum near Tian'anmen Square today.

This sentence structure is also used to describe the occurrence of an incident that is described by a sentence. For example:

几个员工还在工作。
Several employees are still working.
Key words: 员工 employee 工作 to work

办公室里有几个员工还在工作。
There are several employees still working in the office.
Key words: 办公室 office 里 in, inside

一个老人在看书。
An old man is reading.
Key words: 一个老人 an old man 看书 reading

在阳台上有一个老人在看书。
There is an old man reading a book on the balcony.
Key words: 在 in, at, on 阳台 balcony 上 on, up

司机来开车送你到那。
A driver will come to take you there.
Key words: 司机 driver 来 to come 开车 to drive 送 to send

一会儿会有司机来开车送你到那。
There will be a driver coming to take you there.
Key words: 一会 later 开车 to drive 送 to send

几个外国客人来参观我们公司。
Several guests from abroad will come visit our company.
Key words: 外国 foreign 客人 guest 参观 to visit 公司 corporation, company

明天会有几个外国客人来参观我们公司。
There will be several guests from abroad visiting our company tomorrow.

Chapter 5 Sentence Construction

> **Comparing:**
>
> Sentence 1:
> 在瀑布边有很多游客在拍照。
> There are many tourists taking photos near the waterfall.
>   Key words: 瀑布 waterfall 边 aside 游客 tourist 拍照 to take photo
>
> Sentence 2:
> 在瀑布边很多游客在拍照。
> Many tourists are taking photos near the waterfall.

At the same time, the sentences structured in DE-1 can also be integrated into other sentences. For example:

桌子的抽屉里还有两千块钱。
There are 2,000 dollars in the desk drawer.
Key words: 桌子 desk, table 抽屉 drawer 两千 two thousand

我知道桌子的抽屉里还有两千块钱。
I know that there are 2,000 dollars in the desk drawer.

在湖里有条船。
There is a boat on the lake.
Key words: 湖 lake 里 in 条 quantifier for ship 船 boat

他注意到在湖里有条船。
He noticed that there was a boat on the lake.
Key words: 他 he, him 注意到 to notice, to find 湖 lake 里 in 条 quantifier for ship 船 boat

下个月这个剧院会有精彩的歌剧。
There will be a wonderful opera in this opera house next month.
Key words: 下个月 next month 在 at, in, on 剧院 opera house 精彩 wonderful 歌剧 opera

我知道下个月这个剧院会有精彩的歌剧。
I know that there will be a wonderful opera in this opera house next month.

明天会有几个外国客人参观我们公司。
Several guests from abroad will come visit our company tomorrow.

明天会有几个外国客人参观我们公司让我们很紧张。
It makes us a little nervous that several guests from abroad will come visit our company tomorrow.

Chapter 5 Sentence Construction

In addition to the sentences structured with 有, there is another way to make a more vivid description of the existence of a certain subject. If a subject appear in a specific state, we can also use a word that specifically describes that state to substitute 有. The typical sentence structure is:

time + location + state of the subject + subject
Structure code: DE (Description of the Existence) -2

The following illustrates the basic mechanism. For example, there is a pretty girl sitting under a tree, and we can describe the whole scene with two independent sentences:

大树下面有一个漂亮女孩。
There is a pretty girl under the tree.
Key words: 大树 tree 下面 under, beneath 漂亮 pretty 女孩 girl

她在坐着。
She is sitting.
Key words: 她 she, her 坐着 (to be sitting)

Because 坐着 (be sitting) describes her state in appearance, we can then create a simple and vivid description:

大树下面坐着一个漂亮的女孩。
There sits a beautiful girl under the tree.

This structure is used in daily language, and the key to creating such sentences is to find an appropriate word for the specific state. More examples include:

桌子下倒着几个空瓶子。
There are several empty bottles lying under the table.
Key words: 倒 to fall 空 empty 瓶子 bottle

街道上走着几个行人。
There are several passers-by walking along the avenue.
Key words: 街道 street, avenue 上 on, up 走 to walk 几个 several 行人 passer-by

他的书桌上摊着一本英汉字典。
There is an English-Chinese dictionary laid open on his desk.
Key words: 摊 to lay open 本 quantifier for books 英汉字典 English-Chinese dictionary

缆车售票处围着很多人。
There are many people surrounding the cable car ticket office.
Key words: 缆车 cable car 售票处 ticket office 围 to surround 很多 many 人 people

Chapter 5 Sentence Construction

If two sentences have the same subject, they can be integrated into one sentence according to a certain logical sequence. For example, the following two sentences talk about the same subject 快件(an express mail):

桌子上有个快件。
There is an express mail on the desk.
Key words: 桌子 desk 上 on, above 快件 express mail

快件是你的。
The express mail is for you.
Key words: 快件 express mail 你的 your, yours

We can integrate the above two sentences into one:

桌子上有个快件是你的。
There is an express mail for you on the desk.

Other examples:

在门口有个女孩找你。
There is a girl looking for you at the gate.
Key words: 门口 gate 女孩 girl 找 to look for 你 you

街上有几个警察在巡逻。
There are several policemen patrolling the street.
Key words: 街 street 警察 policeman 巡逻 patrol

有架飞机向东飞去。
There is an airplane heading east.
Key words: 架 quantifier for airplane 飞机 airplane 向 towards 东 east 飞去 to fly away

这个公司里有几个新产品达到世界一流水平。
Several new products from this company are among the best in the world.
Key words: 公司 corporation 几个 several 达到 to arrive 一流 first class 水平 level

没有, 没 and 无 are the most commonly used words to express negative meanings. For example:

现在地球上没有恐龙.
There are no dinosaurs on the earth now.
Key words: 现在 now 地球 earth, globe 上 up, above 恐龙 dinosaur

下午办公室里没人.
There is nobody in the office this afternoon.
Key words: 下午 afternoon 办公室 office 人 people

工程目前尚无进展.
There is no progress on the project now.
Key words: 工程 project 目前 now; at present time 尚 still, yet 进展 advance, progress

到现在为止他们无任何成功的可能性。
There was no possibility for them to succeed until now.
Key words: 到现在为止 till now 任何 any 成功 to succeed 可能性 possibility

The following structure is also frequently used for negative descriptions:

Examples:

在办公室里一个人也没有。
There is nobody in the office.
Key words: 在 at, in, on 办公室 office 一个 one 人 people

这几天一点他的消息都没。
There is no news about him recently.
Key words: 这几天 recent days 他 he, him 消息 news, message

这三天一点进展都没有。
There has been no progress the past 3 days.
Key words: 这三天 in the past 3 days

在午夜的大街上一辆出租车都没有。
There are no taxis on the street at midnight.
Key words: 午夜 midnight 大街 street 出租车 taxi

The above structure can also be applied to other sentence structures for negative meanings. For example:

昨天一个人也没来。
Nobody came yesterday.
Key words: 昨天 yesterday 一个人 one person 来 to come

今天上午我没接到他一个电话。
I did not receive a phone call from him this morning.
Key words: 今天 today 上午 morning 我 I, me 他 he, him 电话 phone call 接到 to receive

我们现在连最简陋的工具都没有。
Now we do not have any tools, not even crude ones.
Key words: 最 most 简陋 simple and crude 工具 tool

Chapter 5 Sentence Construction

他的父母对他一点信心也没有。
His parents have no confidence in him.
Key words: 父母 parents 信心 confident; confidence

 Key Application: Specifying a Location

People are used to giving names to cities, mountains, rivers, lakes, and buildings. The following characters are commonly used in naming locations and places in China.

洲 continent	国 country	州 state	省 state
市 city	城 city	县 county	乡 county
镇 county	村(村庄) village	区 district	街道 street, road
路 street, road	巷 alley	里 inner	堡 fortress
寨 village	营 camp	苑 garden	门 gate
胡同 bystreet	条 lane	场 field	堂 hall
馆 hall	所 branch	院 yard	厅 hall
大厦 edifice	中心 center	阁 pavilion	亭 pavilion
宫 palace	庭 court	观 Taoist temple	寺 temple
庙 temple	居 house	园 garden	处 place
洞 cavity	坛 altar	关 pass	坟 tomb
陵 mausoleum	山 mountain	岭 range	峰 summit
崖 cliff	坡 slope	口 cross	沟 channel
洼 low-lying place	江河 river	湖 lake	海 sea
港（津、渡）port	湾 bay, gulf	滩 beach	潭 pond
楼 (a) storied building		祠 ancestral temple	

Some special words for abstract locations are usually combined with the specific locations to provide a more detailed positioning in the description. The most commonly used are:

东 east   南 south   西 west   北 north
内（里）inner   外 outer

Examples:

天安门东 east of Tian'anmen
建国门北 north of Jianguo Men
朝阳门内 inner of Chaoyangmen
复兴门外 outer of Fuxingmen

In addition, 面 (side), 边 (side), 方 (direction), 侧 (side), 部 (section) are also frequently used in demonstrating a location or a direction. For example:

东面 east side   南面 south side   西方 the western area   东北面 northeast side

The above words can also be combined with words that refer to abstract positions and directions, such as 上 (up), 下 (down), 左 (left), 右 (right), 内 (inner), 外 (outer), 前 (front), 后 (rear) etc., to describe more detailed positions and directions. For example:

上面 upper side	中部 middle part	下边 lower part (of)
左方 the left	左侧 left side	后方 rear part (of)
前边 the front	后边 the behind	

Section 5: Special Structures

In this section, we will introduce several special sentence structures.

1. To emphasize initiative

There are two basic sentence structures frequently used to emphasize the initiative of an action:

1. When it is unnecessary or impossible to specify the subject that performs the action, we can simplify the structure as follows:

把(将)+ **subject influenced** + **action**
Structure code: EI (Emphasizing initiative) -1

2. When the subject should be specified, the sentence structure is:

subject that performs an action+把(将) + **subject influenced** + **action**
Structure code: EI (Emphasize initiativeness) -2

This sentence structure is derived from the structure of DA (1, 2). Such sentences are also frequently used in making orders or suggestions. For example:

我们最终把他找到了。
We finally found him.
Key words: 我们 we, us 最终 finally 找到 to find, to discover

你刚才把我吓坏了.
You frightened me to death just now.
Key words: 你 you 刚才 really 吓 to frighten 坏 badly, deadly

一个小时后汽车把我们拉到了一个旅馆。
The car drove us to a hotel an hour later.
Key words: 一个小时后 one hour later 汽车 car 拉 to carry, to drive 到 to reach 旅馆 hotel

在进场前请将手机关闭。
Please turn off your mobile phone before entering.
Key words: 在 at, on, in 进场 to enter 手机 mobile phone 关闭 to turn off

请将填好的表格放在那边桌子上的箱子里。
Please put the completed form into the box on that table over there.
Key words: 填 to fill 表格 sheet 放 to lay, to place 桌子 table 箱子 box 里 in, inside

Chapter 5 Sentence Construction

The key point to remember in creating such sentences is that a basic word for an action cannot be placed at the end of the sentence. For example, we cannot say:

昨天我把书看。×

Note: You can find this structure in some ancient literary works, especially in the lyrics of traditional dramas.

The word that describes the action should indicate a result or a state related to that action. In the above example, we can add 了 after 看 to indicate that the action has already been completed.

我把书看。×
我把书看了。√

Most of the complex words for actions constructed in AS-3 can be used in this structure. For example:

你要把钱藏好。
You should hide your money well.
Key words: 你 you 钱 money 藏 to hide 好 good; well

我得把他的情况摸清楚。
I should find some clear-cut information about him.
Key words: 得 should, need 情况 information 摸 to find, to touch 清楚 clear; clearly

明天老师会把我们这学期的成绩公布出来。
Tomorrow the teacher will post our grades for this semester.
Key words: 老师 teacher 我们 we, us 学期 semester 成绩 grade 公布 to publicize 出来 out

马上把你知道的情况讲出来!
Tell me everything you know immediately!
Key words: 马上 immediately; at once 情况 situation, information 讲 to talk, to speak

If a basic word has to be placed at the end of the sentence, it should be put into a special structure. In the previous chapters, we have discussed several special structures for constructing complex word for actions:

你需要帮忙就说一声。
Tell me if you need help.
Key words: 你 you 要 should 这个问题 this problem 解决 to settle down
Key step: 解决一下 quantity-quantifier structure of an action

你要把这个问题解决一下。
You should solve this problem.

115

Chapter 5 Sentence Construction

Key words: 你 you 要 should 这个问题 this problem 解决 to solve; to settle down
Key step: 解决一下 quantity-quantifier structure of an action

现在赶快把房间收拾收拾!
Clean the room quickly now!
Key words: 现在 now 赶快 quickly 房间 room 收拾 to clean, to trim

你最好尽快把我要的文件准备准备。
You had better get the files I want ready as soon as possible.
Key words: 最好 had better 尽快 as soon as possible 我 I, me 要 to want 准备 to prepare

Each component in EI (1, 2) can be extended into a complicated form. For example:

我把汽车卖掉了。
I sold my car.

大家觉得我把汽车卖掉了很不明智。
Everybody thought that it was unwise for me to sell my car.
Key words: 大家 everyone 觉得 to think 很 very 不 not 明智 wise

他把自己关在了房间里。
He locked himself in the room.
Key words: 他 he, him 自己 oneself 关 to close, to shut 在 at, in, on 房间 room 里 inside

他把自己关在了房间里让他妈妈很不安。
It made his mother very nervous when he locked himself in the room.
Key words: 让 to make 妈妈 mom 很 very 不安 nervous

他能把这个工作按时做完。
He can finish this work on time.
Key words: 他 he, him 能 can 这个工作 this work 按时 on time 做完 to finish

我们不相信他能把这个工作按时做完。
We do not believe that he can finish this work on time.
Key words: 我们 we 不 not, no 相信 to believe

我把他的名字忘记了。
I forgot his name.
Key words: 我 I, me 他 he, him 名字 name 忘记 to forget

我把他的名字忘记了让我很尴尬。
I was embarrassed when I forgot his name.
Key words: 让 to make 很 very 尴尬 embarrassed

不把(不将), 没把(没将), 别把(别将, 勿将, 莫把, 莫将) are frequently added before the words for action to express negative meanings. For example:

请勿将头手伸出车外。
Please do not stick your head or hands outside the vehicle.
Key words: 请 please　头 head　手 hand　伸 to extend　出 out　车 vehicle　外 out

请别把这个消息告诉她。
Please do not tell her this news.
Key words: 消息 message, news　告诉 to tell

邮递员没把包裹及时送给我。
The mail carrier did not deliver the package to me in time.
Key words: 邮递员 postman　包裹 package　及时 in time　送 to send　给 to　我 I, me

这个高层管理者不把下属的意见当回事。
This senior manager would never listen to suggestions from his underlings.
Key words: 高层 senior　管理者 manager　下属 underling　当回事 to pay attention to

Note: generally speaking, 不把 implies unwillingness, 没把（没将）is typically a plain description of a fact, and 别把（别将）is more often than not used to stop someone from doing something.

2. To emphasize the result

To emphasize the influence of an action, we can use the following structure:

subject that issues an action +让+**subject influenced**+**description of the result**
Structure code: ER (Emphasize Result)

Note: In addition to 让, 令, 叫, 使 and 使得 are also frequently used in this structure.

Examples:

这个难题让他很头疼。
This problem gives him a headache.
Key words: 这个 this　难 difficult　题 question　他 he, him　很 very　头疼 headache

持续了好几天的坏天气令我们的旅游计划泡汤了。
The bad weather the last several days spoiled our travel plans.
Key words: 持续 to continue　好几天 several days　旅游 travel　计划 plan

这个餐厅的独特菜肴叫顾客很满意。
The unique dishes in this restaurant please the customers.
Key words: 餐厅 restaurant　独特 unique, special　菜肴 dish　顾客 customer　满意 satisfied

他的诚恳和大度使他很受欢迎。
His sincerity and generosity make him welcomed.
Key words: 诚恳 sincerity 和 and 大度 generosity 很 very 受欢迎 (to be) welcomed

Each component in ER can also be extended to a complicated form. For example:

他轻松地搞定了他的麻烦。
He tackled his trouble easily.
Key words: 他 he, him 轻松 easily 搞定 to resolve, to tackle 他的 his 麻烦 trouble

他轻松地搞定了他的麻烦让我们很惊讶。
It really surprised us that he tackled his trouble so easily.
Key words: 惊讶 surprised

我在演讲中读错了几个字。
I misread several words during my speech.
Key words: 我 I, me 在 at, in, on 演讲 speech 读 to read 错 wrong 几个 several 字 word

我在演讲中读错了几个字使得听众笑出来。
It made the audience laugh when I misread several words during my speech.
Key words: 听众 audience 笑出来 to laugh out

他的举动让我们费解。
His behavior confuses us.
Key words: 他的 his 举动 behavior 我们 we, us 费解 confused

他自己也知道他的举动让我们费解。
He also knows that his behavior confuses us.
Key words: 他 he, him 自己 oneself 也 also, too 知道 to know

良好的工作环境会让员工很勤勉。
A good work environment will result in diligent employees.
Key words: 良好 good 工作 work 环境 environment 员工 employee 勤勉 diligent

最近的调查显示良好的工作环境会让员工很勤勉。
The latest investigation shows that a good work environment results in diligent employees.
Key words: 最近 the latest, recent 调查 investigation 显示 to show, to display

没, 没有, 不, 未 are frequently added before 让 to make negative expressions. For example:

坏天气没有让来这里的游人止步。
The bad weather did not stop the tourists coming here.
Key words: 坏天气 bad weather 游人 tourist 止步 to stop, to quit

他的荣誉没有让他得意。
His honor does not make him self-righteous.
Key words: 他的 his 荣誉 honor 得意 proud

工作的成就并不让我感到幸福。
My success at work does not make me happy.
Key words: 工作 work, job 成就 success, achievement 感到 to feel 幸福 happy

她的新装束没让我们太吃惊。
Her new dress does not surprise us much.
Key words: 她的 her 新 new 装束 dressing 我们 we, us 吃惊 to surprise

3. To emphasize passiveness

There are two basic structures frequently used to emphasize that a subject is passively influenced by another:

1. If it is not necessary to specify the subject that performs an action, we use the following structure:

subject influenced+被+ **action**
Structure code: EP (Emphasize Passiveness) -1

2. When the subject that performs an action is specified, the sentence structure should be:

subject influenced+被+ **subject that issues an action** + **action**
Structure code: EP (Emphasize Passiveness) -2

Note: 给，叫，让 are also frequently used instead of 被 in spoken language.

For example:

这名学者被认为是个权威。
This scholar is regarded as an authority.
Key word: 名 quantifier for people 学者 scholar 认为 to think, to regard 权威 authority

我的数码相机叫我弟弟弄坏了。
My younger brother broke my digital camera.
Key words: 我的 my 数码 digital 相机 camera 我弟弟 my younger brother 弄坏 to break

他的故事很快就让报纸报道了。
The newspapers soon reported on his story.
Key words: 他的 his 故事 story 很快 soon 报纸 newspaper 报道 to report

Chapter 5 Sentence Construction

这部小说给翻译成了很多种语言。
This novel was translated into many languages.
Key words: 部 quantifier for artworks 小说 this novel 翻译 to translate 语言 language

Note: A basic word for action cannot be placed at the end of a sentence in EI (1, 2). The same principle also pertains for EP (1, 2).

Each component in EP (1, 2) can be extended into a complicated form. For example:

昨天我没有上班。
I did not go to work yesterday.
Key words: 昨天 yesterday 我 I, me 上班 to go to work

昨天我没有上班被老板发现了。
My boss found out I did not go to work yesterday.
Key words: 老板 boss 发现 to discover, to find

过去几年这家工厂一直向河里排放污水。
This factory had been draining polluted water into the river over the past several years.
Key words: 工厂 factory 一直 always 河里 in the river 排放 to drain 污 dirty 水 water

过去几年这家工厂一直向河里排放污水被媒体曝光了。
The mass media exposed this factory for draining polluted water into the river over the past several years.
Key words: 媒体 mass media 曝光 to expose

他在度假时经常被同事打扰。
His colleagues frequently disturbed him when he was on vacation.
Key words: 在度假时 (to be) in vacation 经常 usually 同事 colleague 打扰 to disturb

他很恼火他在度假时经常被同事打扰。
He is very angry that his colleagues disturbed him so frequently when he was on vacation.
Key words: 恼火 (to be) angry at

这个工厂很快要被拆掉。
This factory will be dismantled soon.
Key words: 这个工厂 this factory 很快 soon 要 will, should 拆掉 to dismantle

董事会宣布这个工厂很快就要被拆掉。
The board of directors announced that this factory would be dismantled soon.
Key words: 董事会 the board of directors 宣布 announce

没被, 别被, 不被, 勿被 or 莫被 are frequently added to express a negative meaning. For example:

120

Chapter 5 Sentence Construction

你别被胜利冲昏头脑。
Do not let a little success go to your head.
Key words: 胜利 victory 冲昏头脑 to lose one's head

他的那些小把戏还没被揭穿。
His tricks have not yet been exposed.
Key words: 他的 his 那些 those 小把戏 trickery 揭穿 to debunk, to expose

很多创新开始并不被人们重视。
Many inventions were not publicly recognized in the beginning.
Key words: 创新 invention 开始 in the beginning 重视 to attach importance to

当你做决定时勿被表面现象迷惑。
Do not be fooled by appearances.
Key words: 当…时 when… 决定 decision 表面 surface 现象 phenomenon 迷惑 to delude

> **Comparing:**
>
> 没被 is typically used for the description of a fact;
> 不被 usually implies a subjective attitude；
> 别被, 勿被 and 莫被 are more often than not used in making suggestions or warnings, with the last two words frequently used with a more literary style.

4. To emphasize something with …是…的

The sentence structure with …是 …的 is frequently used to emphasize a specific component in a sentence. The following examples show how to use these.

Note: In Chapter 5 Section 3, we have introduced the sentence structure DC-4. However, DC-4 can only be regarded as an abbreviated structure.

Below is a sentence structured according to DA-1:

我昨天在学校门口偶然遇到校长了。
I met the principal by chance at the school gate yesterday.
Key words: 学校门口 gate of the school 偶然 by chance 校长 principal

If we want to emphasize that it was I that met the principal, we can add 是 before the component to be emphasized (我), and then add 的 at the end of the sentence.

The completed sentence is then restructured, from DA-1 into DC-3. At the same time, 了 (a word indicating tense) should be omitted. The new sentence would appear as:

Chapter 5 Sentence Construction

是我昨天在学校门口偶然遇到校长的。
I was the one who met the principal by chance at the school gate yesterday.

With this mechanism, we can easily emphasize various components in the sentence. For example:

我是昨天在学校门口偶然遇到校长的。
It was yesterday that I met the principal by chance at the school gate.

我昨天是在学校门口偶然遇到校长的。
It was at the school gate that I met the principal by chance yesterday.

我昨天在学校门口是偶然遇到校长的。
It was by chance that I met the principal at the school gate yesterday.

If we want to emphasize it was the principal that I met, we cannot say:

我昨天在学校门口遇到是校长的。

To emphasize the subject that is influenced by an act, we should add 的 after the action and add 是 before the subject. Therefore, the correct formulation should be:

我昨天在学校门口遇到的是校长。
It was the principal that I met at the school gate yesterday.

Other examples:

汤姆跟杰克昨天从北京坐飞机到上海去开会。
Tom and Jack flew from Beijing to Shanghai for a meeting yesterday.
Key words: 汤姆 Tom 跟 with; and 杰克 Jack 从北京 from Beijing 坐飞机 to take the airplane 到上海 to Shanghai 去 to go for 开会 to have a meeting

汤姆跟杰克昨天从北京坐飞机到上海去开会的。
Tom was the one who flew with Jack from Beijing to Shanghai for a meeting yesterday.

汤姆是跟杰克昨天从北京坐飞机到上海去开会的。
Jack was the one that Tom flew with from Beijing to Shanghai for a meeting yesterday.

汤姆跟杰克是昨天从北京坐飞机到上海去开会的。
It was yesterday that Tom and Jack flew from Beijing to Shanghai for a meeting.

汤姆跟杰克昨天是从北京坐飞机到上海去开会的。
It was from Beijing that Tom and Jack flew to Shanghai for a meeting yesterday.

汤姆跟杰克昨天从北京是坐飞机到上海去开会的。

Chapter 5 Sentence Construction

It was by air that Tom and Jack went from Beijing to Shanghai for a meeting yesterday.

汤姆跟杰克昨天从北京坐飞机是到上海去开会的。
It was to Shanghai that Tom and Jack flew from Beijing for a meeting yesterday.

汤姆跟杰克昨天从北京坐飞机到上海是去开会的。
It was for a meeting that Tom and Jack flew from Beijing to Shanghai yesterday.

In sentences structured in DE (1, 2), we can indicate whether the emphasis is on the entire meaning or only on the subject. In the first case, we can add 是 before 有 (or the words specifically adopted to describe the state). For example:

在桌子上有几本书。
There are several books on the desk.
Key words: 在 at, in, on 桌子 table 上 up 几本书 several books

在桌子上是有几本书。
Several books are on the desk.

床上躺着一个病人。
There lies a patient in bed.
Key words: 床上 in the bed 躺 to lie 一个病人 a patient

床上是躺着一个病人。
A patient is lying in bed.

In the second case, we can put 的 after 有 (or the words describing the state), and then put 是 before the words for the subject. For example:

在桌子上有的是几本书
On the desk are several books.

床上躺着的是一个病人。
In the bed lies a patient.

For the sentences structured in DC-1, we can also make an emphasis on the various components. For example:

这道菜很好吃。
This dish is very delicious.
Key words: 这道菜 this dish 很 very 好吃 delicious

是这道菜很好吃。
It is this dish that is very delicious.

Chapter 5 Sentence Construction

这道菜是很好吃的。
This dish is the one that is very delicious.

这家商店的东西很便宜。
The things in this shop are very cheap.
Key words: 这家商店 this shop 东西 item, thing 很 very 便宜 cheap

是这家商店的东西很便宜。
It is in this shop that the things are very cheap.

这家商店的东西是很便宜的。
The things in this shop are very cheap.

For sentences structured with 把, 被 and 让, we can make a similar emphasis. The position of 是 helps mark the components that are emphasized. For example:

他的妈妈把他的网球拍借给我了。
His mom lent his tennis racket to me.
Key words: 他的 his 妈妈 mom 网球拍 tennis racket 借 to lend 给 to 我 I, me

是他的妈妈把他的网球拍借给我了。
His mom was the one who lent his tennis racket to me.

他的妈妈是把他的网球拍借给我了。
His mom did lend his tennis racket to me.

楼梯被杂物阻塞了。
Some miscellaneous items blocked the stairway.
Key words: 楼梯 stairway 杂物 odds and ends 阻塞 to block

是楼梯被杂物阻塞了。
This stairway is the one blocked by some miscellaneous items.

楼梯是被杂物阻塞了。
The stairway was blocked by some miscellaneous items.

导游让我们六点起床。
The tour guide asked us to get up at 6 o'clock.
Key words: 导游 tour guide 我们 we, us 六点 6 o'clock 起床 get up

是导游让我们六点起床的。
The tour guide is the one who asked us to get up at 6 o'clock.

导游是让我们六点起床。
The tour guide did ask us to get up at 6 o'clock.

Up to now, we have discussed the most commonly used sentence structures, below is a list for quick reference.

Structure	Code
action preferred to be accomplished	OS-1
subject talked about + action preferred to be accomplished	OS-2
subject that performs an action + action	DA-1
subject that performs an action + action + subject influenced	DA-2
description or comment	DC-1
subject talked about + description or comment	DC-2
subject + 是 + description or comment	DC-3
subject + 是 + description or comment + 的	DC-4
time + location + 有 + subject	DE-1
time + location + state of the subject + subject	DE-2
把(将) + subject influenced + action	EI-1
subject that performs an action + 把(将) + subject influenced + action	EI-2
subject that performs an action + 让 + subject influenced + description of the result	ER
subject influenced + 被 + action	EP-1
subject influenced + 被 + subject that performs an action + action	EP-2
...是...的	ME

Chapter 5 Sentence Construction

 Quick Reference

Here is a list of commonly used structures for the descriptions of locations.

在 + location at, in, on	在中国 in China 在房间 in the room
从(自，打) + location from	从办公室 from the office 打天上 from the sky
到(至,往) + location to	到北京 to Beijing 到学校 to school
从(自，打) + location 1 + 到 (至,往) + location 2 from location 1 to location 2	从地球到月球 from the earth to the moon 自天空至海洋 from the sky to the sea 打南往北 from the south to the north
朝(向，往) + location towards	朝南 towards the south 往北 towards the north

To indicate a more specific position, we usually add a word such as 上, 下, 中, 内, etc., at the end of the structure. For example:

在桌子上 on the table   在桌子下 under the table   从树上 from the tree
到房间里 into the room   从天花板上到地板上 from the ceiling to the floor

We can put any subject into the above structures as long as the subject can have a position or a boundary. For example:

从心底高兴   be happy from the bottom of one's heart
放到手心里   grasp in one's hand
从大人到小孩   from adults to kids
朝我走   walk toward me
飞向未来   fly toward the future

Chapter 6
Specifying Tenses

This chapter covers ways to indicate various tenses in the Chinese language. There are three main methods:

1. Add specific words to function as indicators for tenses.

2. A shared understanding of the background also helps specify the tenses.

3. Use of the above two basic methods can specify some complex tenses.

The following shows the basic skills for specifying the four main tenses:

1. To indicate that something happened in the past

了 is most frequently added after the words for actions to indicate that something happened in a past time. For example:

他去办公室。
He goes to the office.
Key words: 他 he, him 去 to go 办公室 office

他去了办公室。
He went to the office.

他去办公室了。
He went to the office.

> **Comparing:**
>
> Sometimes, the position of 了 makes a subtle difference to the meaning of a sentence. As a rule, when 了 is added directly after the basic word for an action, it emphasizes that the specific action has already happened. When 了 is added after a complete description of an action (usually expressed by a complicated combination), it emphasizes that a certain incident happened. For example:
>
> 刚才警察处罚了出租车司机。(emphasis on the action)
> The police fined the taxi driver just now.
>
> 刚才警察处罚出租车司机了。(emphasis on the whole incident)
> Just now the police fined the taxi driver.

Chapter 6 Specifying Tenses

More examples:

上个礼拜我感冒了。
I caught a cold last week.
Key words: 上个礼拜 last week 我 I, me 感冒 to catch a cold

天气明显暖和了。
The weather turned warm.
Key words: 天气 weather 明显 obvious; obviously 暖和 to warm up

我不小心把事情搞砸了。
I spoiled the job with my carelessness.
Key words: 我 I, me 不小心 carelessly 事情 matter 搞砸 to ruin

上飞机前他的行李被彻底检查了一下。
His luggage was checked thoroughly before he got on the airplane.
Key words: 飞机 airplane 行李 luggage 彻底 thoroughly 检查一下 to have a check

他的所作所为彻底让我失望了。
What he did was thoroughly disappointing.
Key words: 所作所为 things that somebody does 彻底 thoroughly 失望 (to be) disappointed

A shared or mutual background also helps to specify a tense. When common sense indicates that an incident happened in the past, no extra word is required to help specify the tense. For example:

地球大约形成于46亿年前。
The earth came into being about 4.6 billion years ago.
Key words: 地球 earth 大约 about 形成 to form; to come into being

第二次世界大战在1945年结束。
World War II ended in 1945.
Key words: 第二次 second time 世界 world 战 fight, war 结束 to end

我在一九七五年出生。
I was born in 1975.
Key words: 我 I, me 在 at, in, on 一九七五年 the year of 1975 出生 born

这个作家成名于九十年代末。
This author became famous at the end of the 1990s.
Key words: 这个作家 this author 成名 to become famous 于 at 九十年代 1990s 末 end

This mechanism can also be extended to universal cases. If a past time is indicated (or implied) in language, 了 is not always necessary. For example:

Chapter 6 Specifying Tenses

昨天他去医院看(了)他的朋友。
He went to see his friend in the hospital.
Key words: 昨天 yesterday 去 to go 医院 hospital 看 to see, to watch 他的 his 朋友 friend

邻居看到(了)他从家开车出门(了)。
His neighbor saw him driving off from his house.
Key words: 邻居 neighbor 看到 to see, to find 开车 to drive 出门 to go out of home

他知道(了)自己会赢。
He knew that he would win.
Key words: 知道 to know 自己 oneself 赢 to win

昨天下(了)一天雨。
It rained the whole day yesterday.
Key words: 昨天 yesterday 下 to fall 雨 rain

Note: In most cases, it is better to use 了 to make a distinct and accurate description.

没 (没有) or 不 is frequently added before the action to express a negative expression. 了 should be omitted during this formulation. For example:

上周日我没(没有)去上班。
I did not go to work last Sunday.
Key word: 上周日 last Sunday 我 I, me 去上班 to go to work

最终父母不相信这幅漂亮的画是他们的女儿画的。
Ultimately, her parents did not believe that their daughter painted the beautiful picture.
Key words: 最终 finally 相信 believe 幅 quantifier for paintings 画 to paint, to draw

他上次的建议没被老板采纳。
The boss did not adopt his last suggestion.
Key words: 他 he, him 上次 last time 建议 suggestion 老板 boss 采纳 to accept, to adopt

大风没有把他的帽子吹跑。
The strong wind did not blow his cap away.
Key words: 大风 strong wind 他的 his 帽子 cap, hat 吹跑 to blow away

In the sentences structured in DC (1, 2, 3, 4), there is no specific word for an action, thus it is not necessary to add 了 to specify tense. In such cases, the tense is inferred from the context. For example:

他很强壮。
He is strong now.
He was strong before.
Key words: 他 he, him 很 very 强壮 strong

Chapter 6 Specifying Tenses

我是这个公司的员工。
I am an employee of this company.
I was an employee of this company.
Key words: 我 I, me 是 be 这个公司 this company 员工 employee

这个事件的影响很大。
The influence of this incident is enormous.
The influence of this incident was enormous.
Key words: 这个事件 this incident 影响 influence 很大 very big

她穿的这身衣服很酷。
The suit she is wearing is very cool.
The suit she was wearing was very cool.
Key words: 她 she, he 穿 to wear 这身衣服 this suit 很 very 酷 cool

To express the negative, 不 should be added before the corresponding component. For example:

过去几个星期里他并不开心。
He was not happy the past few weeks.
Key words: 过去 in the past 星期 week 里 in, within 并 yet, however 开心 happy

你刚买的车不便宜。
The car you bought was not cheap.
Key words: 你 you 刚 just now, recently 买 to buy, to purchase 车 vehicle 便宜 cheap

去年冬天不是太冷。
It was not too cold last winter.
Key words: 去年 last year 冬天 winter 太 too, very 冷 cold

这次争吵不是我挑起的。
It was not I who started the brawl.
Key words: 这次 this time 争吵 quarrel 我 I, me 挑起 start, raise

For sentences structured in DE (1, 2), 了 is not needed to indicate tense. For example:

桌子上有几张名片。
There are several name cards on the desk.
There were several name cards on the desk.
Key words: 桌子 desk 上 on, up 几张名片 several piece of name cards

空气中有股花香的味道。
There is a fragrant smell of flowers.
There was a fragrant smell of flowers.
Key words: 空气 air 花 flower 香 fragrance 味道 smell

Chapter 6 Specifying Tenses

有不少人想参加这次探险活动。
Quite a few people want to join this exploration.
Quite a few people wanted to join this exploration.
Key words: 不少 quite a few 想 want 参加 join 探险 explore 活动 action

在公共汽车车站上站着不少人。
There are quite a few people standing in the bus-station.
There were quite a few people standing in the bus-station.
Key words: 在 at, in, on 公共汽车站 bus station 站 stand 不少 quite a few of 人 people

To express a negative in DE (1, 2), 没 is added before 有 (or the word describing the state). For example:

房间里一个人都没有。
There is nobody in the room.
There was nobody in the room.
Key words: 房间 room 里 in

下午没有汉语口语课。
There is no lecture for spoken Chinese in the afternoon.
There was no lecture for spoken Chinese in the afternoon.
Key words: 下午 afternoon 汉语口语 oral Chinese 课 class, lecture

这里没有你要买的东西。
There is nothing you want to buy here.
There was nothing you wanted to buy here.
Key words: 这里 here 你 you 要 to want 买 to buy 东西 things, items

这个新开的旅店没有住着客人。
There is no guest staying in this new hotel.
There was no guest staying in this new hotel.
Key words: 新 new; newly 开 to open 旅店 hotel 住 to live, to accommodate 客人 guest

2. To indicate something has happened

For the sentences structured in DA (1, 2), EI (1, 2), ER and EP (1, 2), 已经 (已) is frequently added before the word that refers to the action to indicate something has happened. 了 also should be added in this formulation.

For example:

汽车已经到终点站了。
The bus has already arrived at the terminal.
Key words: 汽车 vehicle 到 to reach, to arrive 终点站 terminal

131

Chapter 6 Specifying Tenses

他已经看了这部电影。
He has seen this movie.
Key words: 他 he, him 看 to watch, to see 这部电影 this movie

推销人员已经把广告塞在我的信箱里了。
The salesperson tucked the ads in my mail box.
Key words: 推销人员 salesman 广告 advertisement 塞 to insert 我的 my 信箱 mail box

街道边的垃圾已经被清理干净了。
The rubbish along the street had been cleaned up.
Key words: 街道 street 边 aside, side 垃圾 rubbish 清理 to clean up 干净 neat, clean

To express negative meanings, 没有, 还没 (还没有), 从未 (从未有, 从来没有, 从没有) or 从不 should be added before the corresponding component. 了 should be omitted. For example:

这个房间以前从来没有人住过。
No one has lived in this room.
Key words: 房间 room 以前 before 住 to live, to reside

老师们以前从来没有见过这么乖巧的学生。
The teachers have never seen such a cute student.
Key words: 老师们 teachers 以前 before 见 to see 这么 so 乖巧 cute 学生 student

他从不把别人对他的评价当回事。
He has never been concerned about other people's comments.
Key words: 别人 others 评价 comment, evaluation 当回事 to take consideration of

我们相信他从来没有发表过这样的言论。
We are convinced that he has never spread the word like this.
Key words: 相信 believe 他 he, him 从来 never 发表 to issue 这样 this 言论 words

For sentences structured in DE (1, 2), use 已经 (已) to indicate tense. Sometimes, 了 can be omitted in such sentences. For example:

到现在为止已经有几十个人报名(了)。
So far, tens of people have been registered.
Key words: 到现在为止 till now 几十个人 tens of people 报名 to register

我们分别已有两年多(了)。
It has been more than two years since we departed.
Key words: 我们 we, us 分别 (to be) apart 两年多 more than two years

酒吧里已坐着几个人(了)。
There have been several people already sitting in the bar.

一个小小的船舱里已经挤了几十个人(了)。
There have been tens of people crowded into a small cabin on a ship.
Key words: 一个 one 小小的 very small 船舱 cabin 里 in 挤 crowd 几十个人 tens of people

To express negative meanings, we usually use 从没有 (从来没有, 未有, 从未有) for DE-1 and 从没有 (从来没有, 从未) for DE-2. 过 is frequently, but not always added after 有 (or the words referring to state). 已经 and 了 should be omitted in these formulations. For example:

从来没有人跟我说过这事。
Nobody told me about this matter.
Key words: 跟 to, with 说 to talk, to speak

我们公司从没有(过)你说的那个人。
There has never been anyone like that in our company.
Key words: 我们 we 公司 company 你 you 说 talk, speak 那个人 that one

这个小镇上从未发生(过)这么奇怪的事。
Such a strange thing has never happened in this small town.
Key words: 这个 this 小镇 town 奇怪 strange

我们分手后来从没有他的任何消息。
There has never been any news about him since we parted.
Key words: 分手 apart 任何 any 消息 news, message

已经 (已) is also frequently used to specify this tense in DC(1,2,3,4), and 了 is also necessary in such sentences. For example:

现在我已经很累了。
I am already very exhausted.
Key words: 现在 now 我 I, me 已经 already 很 very 累 tired

现在已经八点了。
It has already been 8 o'clock.
Key words: 现在 now 已经 already 八点 8 o'clock

她已经是他的未婚妻了。
She has already been his fiancée.
Key words: 她 she, her 已经 already 他的 his 未婚妻 fiancée

已经不 or 已经不再 is frequently used to express negative meanings in DC-1 and DC-2. For sentences structured in DC-3 and DC-4, 已经不是 or 已经不再是 is frequently used to indicate a negative meaning. In most cases, 了 should be added in the sentence. For example:

Chapter 6 Specifying Tenses

天气已经不冷了。
It is no longer cold.
Key words: 天气 weather 冷 cold

接下来的工作已经不再困难了。
The work left is no longer difficult.
Key words: 接下来 next 工作 work, job 困难 difficult

你已经不是我们的一员了。
You are no longer one of us.
Key words: 一员 a member of

这些问题已经不再是我能解决的了。
These problems are no longer ones that I can deal with.
Key words: 问题 question, problem 解决 to resolve, to settle

By adopting the specific words for tense and using a context that indicates a past time, we can identify a complex tense demonstrating that something had happened in various sentence structures. For example:

十点钟的时候音乐会就已经结束了。
The concert was already over by 10 o'clock.
Key words: 十点钟的时候 at 10 o'clock 音乐会 concert 结束 to finish, (to be) over

去年八月他已经回中国了。
He was back in China last August.
Key words: 去年 last year 八月 August 他 he 已经 already 回 to return; back to 中国 China

我来的时候客人已经很不高兴了。
The guests were already very unhappy when I arrived.
Key words: 我的来的时候 when I arrived 客人 guest 已经 already 走 to go, to walk

很早以前已经有人探索过这个山洞了。
Someone already explored this cave a long time ago.
Key words: 很早以前 a long time ago 已经 already 探索 to explore 这个山洞 this cave

3. To indicate that something will happen

To indicate this tense in sentences structured in DA, EI, ER, EP, we usually add a specific word to mark the tense. The most commonly used are 会, 要, 将, 将会 and 将要, which should be added before the word for an action. For example:

演出马上就要开始了。
The show will start soon.
Key words: 演出 show 马上 soon 开始 to begin, to start

明天我和我的朋友要去打羽毛球。
My friends and I will play badminton tomorrow.
Key words: 明天 tomorrow 和 and, with 我的朋友 my friends 打 to play 羽毛球 badminton

未来几年政府会大力治理工业污染。
The government will make a strong effort to fight industrial pollution.
Key words: 未来 future 大力 hardly, strongly 治理 to cure 工业 industrial 污染 pollution

你提出的方案将被认真审核。
The plan you proposed will be evaluated thoroughly.
Key words: 你 you 提出 to raise, to propose 方案 plan 认真 seriously 审核 to evaluate

For negative meanings, we usually use 不会 or 将不会 instead of the above words. For example:

他估计不会来。
He probably will not come.
Key words: 估计 probably 来 to come

我绝对不会放过任何机会。
I will never let go of any opportunity.
Key words: 绝对 absolutely 放过 to let go 任何 any 机会 opportunity, chance

短期内事情不会有太多变化。
Things will not change much in a short time.
Key words: 短期内 within a short period 太多 many, much 变化 to change

这些困难将不会让工程的整体进度减缓。
These difficulties will not slow the schedule of the entire project.
Key words: 工程 project 整体 all, whole 进度 progress, schedule 减缓 to slow, to drag

For sentences structured in DC, we usually use 将是, 会是, 将会是 for affirmative meanings, and 不会是 or 将不会是 for negative meanings. For example:

他肯定会是一个很好的丈夫。
Surely he will be a good husband.
Key words: 肯定 sure; surely 一个 one 很好 very 丈夫 husband

这段行程将是很难熬的。
This section of the journey will be tough.
Key words: 这段行程 this section of journey 很 very 难熬 tough, hard

根据天气预报明天的天气不会很差。
According to the forecast, the weather will not be bad.
Key words: 根据 according to 天气预报 weather forecast 明天 tomorrow 很差 very bad

最终成功的人将不会是我的对手。
My opponent will never be the one who wins.
Key words: 最终 finally 成功 to win, to succeed 我的 my, mine 对手 opponent

For sentences structured in DE-1 and DE-2, we add 会 (要, 将, 将会, 将要) before 有 (or the word describing the state of a subject).

For example:

到明年这个大学里会有超过一万名学生。
There will be more than 10,000 students in this university next year.
Key words: 到明年 to next year 这个大学 this university 超过 to exceed

你们到达的时候会有人来接。
There will be someone to meet you when you arrive.
Key words: 到达的时候 when somebody arrives 人 people 来接 meet, to come to receive

下周在这片空地上将铺上一片草坪。
There will be grass covering this open field next week.
Key words: 这片空地 this open field 上 up, on 铺上 to shield, to cover 草坪 grass land

很快这里将弥漫着花香。
The fragrance of flowers will soon fill the air.
Key words: 很快 soon 这里 here 弥漫 to suffuse 花香 fragrance of flower

To express negative meanings, we usually use 没有, 不会有, 将没有 for sentences structured in DE-1, and 不会 (将不会) for those in DE-2.

For example:

一个小时内没有到飞机到达。
There will be no airplane arriving for an hour.
Key words: 一个小时内 within one hour 飞机 airplane 到达 to arrive

三天内不会有新的任务。
There will be no new mission in the next three days.
Key words: 一个小时内 within one hour 飞机 airplane 到达 to arrive

这里将不会出现任何陌生人。
There will be no strangers here.
Key words: 出现 to show, to appear 任何 any 陌生人 stranger, visitor

他们的研究短时间内不会有任何突破。
There will not be any break in their research in the short term.
Key words: 研究 research 短时间内 within a short time 任何 any 突破 breakthrough

Chapter 6 Specifying Tenses

4. To indicate something is (are, was, etc.) going on

For sentences structured in DA, EI, EP, ER, we usually add 正 or 正在 before words referring to an action. For example:

窗户外正飘着雪花。
The snowflakes are floating down outside the window.
Key words: 窗户 window 外 outside 飘 to float, to waft 雪花 snowflake

列车正在进站。
The train is arriving at the platform.
Key words: 列车 train 进 to enter 站 platform

现在我们正在讨论下一步的行动计划。
Now we are discussing the plan for the next movement.
Key words: 现在 now 我们 we, us 讨论 to discuss 下一步 next 行动 action 计划 plan

目前全球气候正变得越来越温暖。
At this time, the global climate is becoming warmer.
Key words: 目前 at present time 全球 world; global 越来越 more and more 温暖 warm

Note: To express the fact that several different actions are (were) happening simultaneously, integrate them into a structure like 一边…一边… (边…边…). For example:

他一边听一边记。
He is making notes as he listens.

回家时我们边走边唱。
We were singing as we walked back home.

By using 正 or 正在 in a context that specifies a past time, we create a complex tense indicating that something was happening. Examples:

去年九月我正在学习汉语。
I was learning Chinese last September.
Key words: 去年 last year 九月 September 学习 learn 汉语 Chinese

刚才他在查阅电子邮件。
He was checking his e-mail just now.
Key words: 刚才 just now 他 he, him 查阅 check, go through 电子邮件 e-mail

下雨时我们正在街上走着。
We were walking on the street when it rained.
Key words: 下雨 to rain 街 street 走 to walk

Chapter 6 Specifying Tenses

上个月他正在一个僻静的小岛上度假。
He was enjoying his vacation on a small isolated island last month.
Key words: 僻静 quiet, isolated 小岛 small island 度假 (to be) on vacation

To express negative meanings for such sentences, use 没在 before the word for action. For example:

现在我没在学习。
I am not studying now.
Key words: 现在 now 我 I, me 学习 to study

我知道几分钟前你们没在开会。
I know that you were not having a meeting several minutes ago.
Key words: 知道 to know 几分钟 several minutes 开会 to have a meeting

上个星期里检查人员没在研究这个问题。
The inspectors were not working on this problem last week.
Key words: 检查人员 inspector 研究 to research, to work 问题 question, problem

当经理进来的时候我们都没在干活。
None of us was working when the manager came in.
Key words: 当...时候 when 经理 manager 进来 to come in 我们 we, us 干活 to work

To indicate this tense for sentences structured in DE-1, use 正有, 正在有. For those in DE-2, place 正, 正在 before the word that describes the state. For example:

现在正有几个人朝我们跑过来。
There are several people running toward us now.
Key words: 现在 now 几个人 several people 朝 to, towards 跑过来 to run to

门口正有一个女孩找你。
There is a girl at the gate looking for you.
Key words: 门口 gate 一个女孩 a girl 找 to find, to seek for 你 you

Note: for the above two sentences, we can also say:

现在有几个人正朝我们跑过来。

门口有一个女孩正在找你。

To specify a complex tense for something that will be happening in the future, use 将在, 会在, 将会在 in a sentence. For example:

十分钟后有个车会在等你。
A car will be waiting for you ten minutes later.
Key words: 分钟 minute 车 car, vehicle 等 to wait

你到他办公室的时候他可能会在见一个重要客户。
He will probably be meeting an important client when you arrive at his office.
Key words: 办公室 office 可能 possibly 见 to meet 重要 important 客户 client

明天中午我会在实验室干点活。
I will be working in the lab at noon tomorrow.
Key words: 明天 tomorrow 中午 noon 实验室 lab 干点活 to do some work

下个月的今天我会在一个遥远的城市游荡。
I will be loafing about in a city far away on this date next month.
Key words: 下个月 next month 遥远 far away 城市 city 游荡 to loaf about, to loiter

Quick Reference

Below is a list of the most popularly used words and phrases for times:

很久以前, 很早以前	a long time ago
以前, 从前	before
前些 + 年(日子, 天)	several years (days) ago
前(头)几个 + 月(星期, 礼拜, 小时, etc.)	several months (weeks, hours, etc.) ago
过些 + 年(日子, 天)	several years (days) later
过几个 + 月(星期, 礼拜, 小时, 钟头, etc.)	several month (weeks, hours, etc.) later
前(头)几 + 年(个月, 天, 个小时)	several years (months, days, hours) before
现在, 目前, 当前, 眼下	at the present time
短时间内, 暂时	in a short time
今后, 以后, 往后, 日后	from now on
过段时间	after a period of time
好几 + 年(个月, 个星期, 个礼拜, 天, etc.)	quite a few of years (months, weeks, days, etc.)
很久, 很长时间	a very long time
一直, 永远, 永久	forever, always

Chapter 7
Raising a Question

Questions can be placed into three types according to their function.

The first type asks for a confirmation, and the answer is usually a "yes" or "no". For example:

你是中国人吗？
Are you Chinese?
Key words: 你 you 是 to be 中国人 Chinese (people)

他完成作业了吗？
Did he finish the homework?
Key words: 他 he, him 完成 to finish 作业 homework

The second type asks for some detailed information. For example:

你昨天晚上几点到的？
When did you arrive last night?
Key words: 你 you 昨天 yesterday 晚上 night 几点 when, what time 到 to arrive

你现在感觉怎么样？
How are you feeling now?
Key words: 你 you 现在 now 感觉 feel 怎么样 how

The third type shows a specific tone or mood. For example:

我不是告诉过你不要迟到吗？
Haven't I told you not to be late?
Key words: 我 I, me 告诉 tell 你 you 不要 should not 迟到 (to be) late

你怎么能这么对我？
How can you treat me like that?
Key words: 你 you 怎么 how 能 can 这么 so; like this 对 to treat 我 me

All questions are based on the normal structures discussed above. To construct a type one question, we simply add a specific word to the sentence; to construct a type two question, we substitute the component to be queried with a corresponding word. For example:

Chapter 7 Raising a Question

他很喜欢那个女孩。
He likes the girl very much.
Key words: 他 he, him 很 very 喜欢 to like, to love 那个女孩 that girl

他很喜欢那个女孩吗？
Does he like the girl very much?

桌子上有三本书。
There are three books on the table.
Key words: 桌子上 on the desk 三本书 three books

桌子上有几本书？
How many books are there on the table?

Chapter 7 Raising a Question

Section 1: Questions Requiring Confirmation

The simplest way to construct a question requiring a "yes" or "no" answer has two steps:
1. Create (or imagine) an affirmative sentence;
2. Add 吗 at the end of the sentence.

Note: Sometimes 吗 can be omitted in spoken language.

您需要帮助吗?
Do you need help?
Key words: 您 you 需要 to need 帮助 help

事故的原因被找到了(吗)?
Have they discovered the reason for the accident?
Key words: 事故 accident 原因 reason, cause

房间里有人吗?
Is somebody in the room?
Key words: 房间 room 里 in 人 people

他把去北京的行程安排好了(吗)?
Has he scheduled his journey to Beijing?
Key words: 去 go 北京 Beijing 行程 journey, schedule 安排 to arrange 好 good; well

你的判断是对的(吗)?
Is your judgment right?
Key words: 你的 your 判断 to judge; judgment 对的 right

啦, rather than 吗, is also frequently used in spoken language. However, for sentences ending with 了, we seldom use 啦 to construct a question. For example:

他戒烟啦?
Did he quit smoking?
Key words: 他 he, him 戒 to quit 烟 cigarette

你看过这部电影啦?
Have you seen this movie?
Key words: 看 to watch, to see 这部电影 this movie

我们真的被他骗啦?
Has he really cheated us?
Key words: 骗 to cheat

Chapter 7 Raising a Question

他的父母送他去国外上学啦？
Did his parents send him abroad to study?
Key words: 父母 parents 送 to send 国外 abroad 上学 to study

In addition to the above simple methods, some other ways are also popularly used:

1. To add a short sentence after a confirmative sentence

We can add an independent short question after an affirmative sentence. The most popularly used ones are:
是吧？
是吗？
是不是？
对吗？
对不对？
对不？

For example:

这部小说很精彩，是吗？
This novel is quite wonderful, isn't it?
Key words: 这部小说 this novel 很 very, quite 精彩 wonderful

你不喜欢喝茶，是不是？
You do not like tea, do you?
Key words: 你 you 喜欢 to like, to love 喝 to drink 茶 tea

他本人不如照片上的好看，对吗？
He is not as handsome as the picture, is he?
Key words: 本人 oneself 不如 less than 照片 picture, photo 好看 pretty, handsome

大家会让你做代表来发言，对不对？
You will be the representative to give a speech, won't you?
Key words: 大家 everybody, all 做 to do 代表 representative 发言 to make a speech

This mechanism can be extended into universal situations. For example:

你明天下午去机场接客人，好不好？
You go to the airport to pick up the guest tomorrow afternoon, OK?
Key words: 下午 afternoon 去 to go 机场 airport 接 to receive, to pick up 客人 guest

这件事我来处理，行吗？
I will take care of this matter, OK?
Key words: 这件事 this matter 来 to come 处理 to handle, to deal

143

Chapter 7 Raising a Question

由你组织一场羽毛球比赛，行不行？
You organize a badminton match, OK?
Key words: 由 by 组织 to organize 羽毛球 badminton 比赛 to match

我们把这点活干完再去吃午饭，可以吧？
We will go to lunch after we finish the work, OK?
Key words: 干完 to finish 再 then 午饭 lunch

没 (没有) is frequently added at the end of sentences structured in DA, EI, ER and EP to form a question for confirmation of whether something has happened or not. For example:

你找到了工作没？
Have you found a job or not?
Key words: 你 you 找到 to find 工作 job

工人把我的汽车修好了没？
Have the workers finished repairing my car or not?
Key words: 工人 worker 我的 my 汽车 car 修好 to repair

房间整理好了没有？
Has the room been cleaned up or not?
Key words: 房间 room 整理 to clean 好 good; well

2. Using a special structure with 不 or 没

For sentences structured in DA, we can use special structures to form a question. The most popular ones are:

A. word for action + 不 (没) + word for action

B. (是) + as word for action + 还是不 (没) + word for action

Examples:

你想不想喝茶？
你(是)想喝茶还是不想？
Do you want some tea or not?
Key words: 你 you 想 to want 喝 to drink 茶 tea

Note: Because 还是 already indicates a question, 吗 is not necessary at the end of the sentence. For the first sentence, we can also say: 你想喝茶不想？

他到底懂不懂你的话？
他到底懂你的话不懂？

144

Chapter 7 Raising a Question

他到底是懂还是不懂你的话？
Did he understand your talk or didn't he?
Key words: 他 he, him 到底 at all 懂 to understand, to comprehend 你的 your 话 word

你喜欢不喜欢她？
你喜欢她不喜欢？
你是喜欢她还是不喜欢？
Do you like her or not?
Key words: 你 you 喜欢 to love, to like 她 she, her

这个事你能不能解决？
这个事你能解决不能？
这个事你能解决还是不能？
Can you handle this matter or not?
Key words: 这个事 this matter 能 can 解决 to settle, to handle

会 and 要 can be put in the above structure. For example:

几个小时后会下雨不会？
几小时后会不会下雨？
几个小时后是会下雨还是不会？
Will it rain in a few hours or not?
Key words: 几个 several 小时 hour 后 after 会 will, can 下雨 to rain

下周你要不要去北京？
下周你要去北京不要？
下周你是要去北京还是不要去？
Will you go to Beijing next week or not?
Key words: 下周 next week 你 you 要 will, should 去 to go 北京 Beijing

In addition to the above, 是不是, 是否 (whether or not) are popularly used in formulating such questions. 是否 usually provides a more literal style. For example:

你昨天是不是已经把工作干完了？
Did you complete your work yesterday?
Key words: 昨天 yesterday 是不是 whether or not 已经 already 工作 work 干完 to finish

这趟公共汽车的路线是否已经被调整了？
Has this bus route been modified?
Key words: 这趟公共汽车 this bus 路线 route 是否 whether or not 调整 to adjust, to modify

For sentences structured in DE, it is possible to adopt the above structures to formulate a question. For example:

昨天下午这里有没有人来过？

145

Chapter 7 Raising a Question

昨天下午这里有人来过没有？
昨天下午这里是有人来过还是没有？
Was there anybody here yesterday afternoon?
Key words: 昨天 yesterday 下午 afternoon 这里 here 人 people 来 to come

一会你会不会有新电子邮件？
一会你会有新电子邮件不会？
一会儿会有新电子邮件还是不会？
Will there be a new e-mail for you in a while?
Key words: 一会 after a while 你 you 会 will, should 新 new 电子邮件 e-mail

现在房间里坐没坐着人？
现在房间里坐着人没有？
现在房间里是坐着人还是没有？
Is there anyone sitting in the room now?
Key words: 现在 now 房间 room 里 in 坐 to sit 人 people

For sentences structured in DC, we typically use 是不是, 是否 to form a question. For example:

外面是不是特别冷？
Is it very cold outside or not?
Key words: 外面 outside 是 to be 特别 very, especially 冷 cold

Note: we can also say 外面是特别冷不是？

我买的这双鞋是不是很贵？
我买的这双鞋是很贵不是？
Was the pair of shoes I bought very expensive or not?
Key words: 我 I, me 买 to buy 这双鞋 this pair of shoes 是 be 很 very 贵 expensive

我们明天早上八点出发是不是有点晚了？
我们明天早上八点出发是否有点晚了？
Will it be too late for us to leave at 8 o'clock tomorrow morning?
Key words: 明天 tomorrow 早上 morning 八点 8 o'clock 出发 to set off 有点 a little 晚 late

还是 (or) is frequently used to list the possible choices of a question. For example:

你们想打排球还是打网球？
Do you want to play volleyball or tennis?
Key words: 打排球 to play volleyball 打网球 to play tennis

你们想打排球，打网球，爬山，还是游泳？
你们想打排球还是打网球，爬山还是游泳？
Do you want to play volleyball, tennis, climb the mountain, or go swimming?

Chapter 7 Raising a Question

Key words: 爬山 to climb the mountain　游泳 to swim

我们应该走这条路还是那条路？
Should we take this road or that one?
Key words: 应该 should　走 to walk　这条路 this road　那条路 that road

我应该把信件交给你还是交给他？
Should I give this letter to you or to him?
Key words: 应该 should　信件 letter　交给 to give to

 Extra Knowledge: Symmetry and Equality

　　In the aesthetics of the Chinese language, people pursue symmetry and equality both in the meanings and in the appearance of the characters. Chinese traditional literary works, such as Chinese couplets and ancient poems, exhibit this gracefulness in their phrasing.

 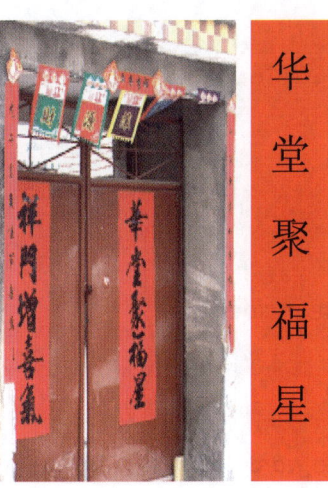 

147

Chapter 7 Raising a Question

Section 2: Questioning Specific Components

To question a specific component in a sentence, such as the time, location, action, etc., we should select a word corresponding to the meaning of the component, and substitute it for the unknown component. The following example shows the basic mechanism in this construct:

昨天邻居的猫在阳台上偷吃了汤姆的两条鱼。
The neighbor's cat stole and ate Tom's two fish on the balcony yesterday.
Key words: 邻居 neighbor 猫 cat 阳台 balcony 偷吃 to steal, to filch 两条鱼 two fish

The above sentence is constructed in DA-2, and the components in the sentence are:

Time:	昨天	yesterday
Location:	阳台上	on the balcony
Subject that performs the action:	邻居的猫	neighbor's cat
The sub-components: owner:	邻居	neighbor
subject:	猫	cat
action:	偷吃	to steal
Object influenced:	汤姆的两条鱼	Tom's two fish
The sub-components: owner:	汤姆	Tom
quantity:	两条	two
quantity:	两条	two
object:	鱼	fish

Suppose that we do not know the time of the incident:

???邻居的猫在阳台上偷吃了汤姆的两条鱼。

To question the time of the incident, we place the word 什么时候 (when) in the sentence to substitute for the unknown component.

什么时候
⬇
???邻居的猫在阳台上偷吃了汤姆的两条鱼。
⬇
什么时候邻居的猫在阳台上偷吃了汤姆的两条鱼？
When did the neighbor's cat steal and eat Tom's two fish on the balcony?

Chapter 7 Raising a Question

A good way to form such a question is to first imagine a sentence for an incident, and then substitute the unknown part with a proper word for inquiry. Here is a brief summary of the words that are popularly used for this:

when, what time	什么时候, 何时, 几时
where	哪, 哪里
who, whom	谁
whose	谁的
what	什么
how	怎么, 如何, 怎样, 多
how much, how many	多少 几
which	哪+ quantifier
why	为什么, 怎么, 怎, 为何

Thus, we can formulate questions for the various components using these substitutions:

哪里

昨天邻居的猫在???偷吃了汤姆的两条鱼。

昨天邻居的猫在哪里偷吃了汤姆的两条鱼？
Where did the neighbor's cat steal and eat Tom's two fish yesterday?

谁

昨天???在阳台上偷吃了汤姆的两条鱼。

昨天谁在阳台上偷吃了汤姆的两条鱼？
Who stole and ate Tom's two fish on the balcony yesterday?

什么

昨天邻居的猫在阳台上偷吃了???。

昨天邻居的猫在阳台上偷吃了什么？
What did the neighbor's cat steal and eat on the balcony yesterday?

Chapter 7 Raising a Question

谁
↓
昨天邻居的猫在阳台上偷吃了 ??? 的两条鱼。
↓
昨天邻居的猫在阳台上偷吃了 谁 的两条鱼？
Whose two fish were stolen and eaten by the neighbor's cat on the balcony yesterday?

谁
↓
昨天 ??? 的猫在阳台上偷吃了汤姆的两条鱼。
↓
昨天 谁 的猫在阳台上偷吃了汤姆的两条鱼？
Whose cat was it that stole and ate Tom's two fish on the balcony yesterday?

怎么
↓
昨天邻居的猫在阳台上 ??? 了汤姆的两条鱼。
↓
昨天邻居的猫在阳台上 怎么 了汤姆的两条鱼？
What did the cat do to Tom's two fish on the balcony yesterday?

干什么
↓
昨天邻居的猫在阳台上 ???。
↓
昨天邻居的猫在阳台上 干什么 了？
What did the neighbor's cat do on the balcony yesterday?

多少（几）
↓
昨天邻居的猫在阳台上偷吃了汤姆的 ??? 条鱼。
↓
昨天邻居的猫在阳台上偷吃了汤姆的 多少（几）条鱼？
How many of Tom's fish did the neighbor's cat steal and eat on the balcony yesterday?

To inquire about a reason for something, we use 为什么 or 怎么 (why) to formulate the question. For example:

为什么汤姆生气了？
汤姆怎么生气了？
Why was Tom angry?

Chapter 7 Raising a Question

Note: 怎么 is rarely placed at the beginning of a sentence.

Alternatively, the question could be phrased:

Tom 生气了，为什么？
Tom was angry, why?

More examples:

去年他什么时候毕业的？
When did he graduate last year?
Key words: 去年 last year 他 he, him 什么时候 when 毕业 to graduate

你打算什么时候把真相说出来？
When will you tell the truth?
Key words: 你 you 打算 to plan 什么时候 when 真相 truth 说 to say, to speak 出来 out

最近的酒店在哪？
Where is the nearest hotel?
Key words: 最近的 nearest 酒店 restaurant 在 (be) at, on, in 哪 where

附近哪有银行？
Where is a bank nearby?
Key words: 附近 nearby 哪 where 银行 bank

是谁把我的自行车骑走了？
Who rode away on my bicycle?
Key words: 是 to be 谁 who 我的 my 自行车 bicycle 骑 to ride 走 to go; away

你把钱交给谁了？
To whom did you give the money?
Key words: 你 you 钱 money 交给 to give to 谁 who, whom

门口那辆时髦的汽车是谁的？
Whose trendy car is that at the gate?
Key words: 门口 gate 那辆时髦的汽车 that trendy car 是 to be 谁的 whose

在你的朋友中谁的电脑最贵？
Who has the most expensive computer among your friends?
Key words: 在 at 朋友 friend 中 among 谁的 whose 电脑 computer 最 most 贵 expensive

他手里的东西是什么？
What is that in his hand?
Key words: 他 he, him 手里 in hand 东西 thing, item 是 to be 什么 what

151

Chapter 7 Raising a Question

我**怎么**能很快的摆脱困境啊？
How can I get out of this mess quickly?
Key words: 怎么 how 能 can 很快 fast, quickly 摆脱 to get rid of 困境 difficulty, mess

我应该**如何**填这张表？
How do I fill out this form?
Key words: 我 I, me 应该 should 如何 how 填 to fill 这张表 this sheet

这块表**多少**钱？
How much is this watch?
Key words: 这块表 this watch 多少 how much 钱 money

你们家有**几**口人？
How many people are there in your family?
Key words: 你们家 your family 几 how many, how much 口 quantifier for people 人 people

这几本书你最喜欢**哪**本？
Which one do you like best among these books?
Key words: 几 several 本 quantifier for books 你 you 最 most 喜欢 to love, to like 哪 which

哪一间房间是我的？
Which room is for me?
Key words: 哪 which 间 quantifier for rooms 房间 room 是 to be 我的 my, mine

你昨天**为什么**不接我的电话？
Why didn't you answer my call yesterday?
Key words: 为什么 why 不 not 接 to answer 我的 my, mine 电话 telephone

这个产品**为什么**受消费者欢迎？
Why is this product so well received by consumers?
Key words: 这个产品 this product 为什么 why 受 to receive 消费者 consumer

Such questions can also be regarded as independent words and be integrated into other sentence structures. For example:

请告诉**我应该如何填这张表**。
Please tell me how to fill out this form.
Key words: 告诉 to tell 应该 should 如何 how 填 to fill 这张表 this sheet

在你的朋友中谁的电脑最贵一直是我们的话题。
We have had an ongoing discussion about whose notebook computer is the most expensive.
Key words: 谁的 whose 电脑 computer 最 most 贵 expensive 一直 always 话题 discussion

没有人知道**哪一间房间是我的**。
Nobody knows which room is mine.

Key words: 没有人 nobody 哪 which 间 quantifier for rooms 房间 room 是 to be

你想知道这个产品为什么受消费者欢迎吗？
Do you want to know why this product is so well received by consumers?
Key words: 知道 to know 产品 product 为什么 why 受 to receive 消费者 consumer

In addition to their basic function in formulating questions, some of the above words are frequently used to refer to abstract and universal concepts.

什么时候, 几时	whenever
哪, 什么地方	wherever
哪 + quantifier	whichever
什么人, 谁	whoever
什么, 任何	whatever

Examples:

什么时候军人都要保持警惕。
The soldiers should stay vigilant whenever it is.
Key words: 什么时候 whenever 军人 soldier 都 all 要 should 保持 to keep 警惕 vigilant

我几时看到他，他总是在忙碌。
He is always busy whenever I see him.
Key words: 几时 whenever 看到 to see, to find 总是 always 忙碌 busy

他到哪都喜欢夸耀自己。
He likes to show off wherever he is.
Key words: 到 to reach 都 all 喜欢 to love, to like 夸耀 to brag, to show off 自己 oneself

我被分配到哪个部门工作都可以。
It will be fine for me to be assigned to whichever department.
Key words: 分配 to assign 哪个 whichever 部门 department 都 all 可以 good, well

谁想要这本书我就把书给谁。
I will give this book to whoever wants it.
Key words: 谁 whoever 想 want 要 to ask for 这本书 this book 就 then 给 to give

他什么新鲜事都喜欢尝试一下。
He likes new experiences whatever they are.
Key words: 什么 whatever 新鲜 fresh 事 thing 都 all 喜欢 to love 尝试一下 to have a try

There are three main types of questions. In the third type, the questions are used to show some specific voice, such as anger, doubt, dissatisfaction, etc. For example:

Chapter 7 Raising a Question

你真的不知道吗？
You really don't know that?
Key words: 真的 really 知道 know

事情会象我们想的那样吗？
Will the business go the way we thought?
Key words: 事情 business, matter 象 like, as 想 to think 那样 that way

你以为他会听你的话？
Do you think that he listens to your advice?
Key words: 以为 to think 听 to listen to

这个办法能行吗？
Does this method really work?
Key words: 办法 way, method 行 to work

你干了些什么？
What have you done?
Key words: 干 to do 事 matter

谁会做这种傻事！
Who(ever) would do such a silly thing!
Key words: 谁 who 会 will, can 做 to do 这种 this kind of 傻 silly 事 thing, matter

你到哪能找到像她那么贤淑的女孩！
Where(ever) can you find a girl as virtuous as she is!
Key words: 到 to reach 哪 where 找到 to find 像 like 那么 so 贤淑 virtuous 女孩 girl

Chapter 7 Raising a Question

 Extra Knowledge: Customs in Raising Questions

In daily language, there are some subtle rules and skills used to formulate questions. For example, in China, when we ask someone's age, we have to choose a specific form that corresponds to his or her specific state and title. For example:

How old are you?

你几岁了？	(to children)
你多大了？	(to young people)
您多大年纪了？	(to an older person)
您贵庚了？	(to older people)
您高寿了？	(to very aged people)
您芳龄多少？	(to young women)

What is your name?

你叫什么名字？	(to people of junior state)
您贵姓？	(a general question)
请问您的尊姓大名？	(to people of senior state)
怎么称呼您？	(a general question)
请问您的芳名是什么？	(to young women)

Chapter 8
Constructing Complex Sentences

The previous chapter introduced some basic skills to help specify the internal structures of complex words. For example, 而 is frequently used to join two parallel meanings:

This mechanism also works in joining various sentences into one complex sentence. Similar to what happens when combining characters, the precondition is that there must be certain logical relations between (or among) the meanings described by the sentences. In most cases, we need to add some specific words (called conjunctions) to indicate the various logical relations. The following example shows the basic mechanism for doing this.

Here are two sentences describing 罗丝 (Rose)'s versatility in sports:

罗丝会游泳。
Rose can swim.

罗丝会打网球。
Rose can play tennis.

We can use 不但 (not only) and 而且 (but also) to integrate the two single sentences into a complex whole:

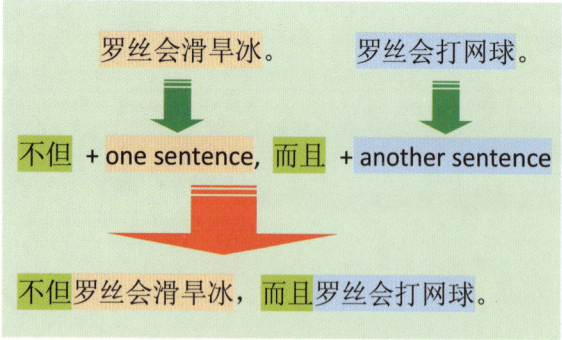

We can create a more compact sentence by consolidating the common words in the two sub-sentences:

Chapter 8 Constructing Complex Sentences

罗丝不但会游泳，而且会打网球。
Rose can not only swim but also play tennis.

Note: Actually, there are many optional words for indicating each type of logical relation. For example, the words function the same as 不但...而且...

不仅...而且...　　不只...而且...　不光...而且...
不但...并且...　　不光...并且...　不只...并且...

More examples:

这道菜不仅好吃而且好看。
This dish is not only tasty but also attractive.
Key words: 这道菜 this dish　好吃 tasty, delicious　好看 nice looking

这套房子不光质量好并且还很便宜。
This suite (of rooms) is not only good quality but also cheap.
Key words: 套 a suite (of rooms)　房子 house　质量 quality　便宜 cheap

现在他不只学习汉语，并且还学习法语。
Now he is not only studying Chinese but also French.
Key words: 现在 now　学习 study　汉语 Chinese　法语 French

我们不仅为你找好了旅行社，而且安排了一个很好的导游。
We not only found a good travel agency but also found a good tour guide for you.
Key words: 为 for　找 to find　旅行社 travel agency　安排 to arrange　导游 tour guide

Below is a list of examples for integrating single sentences into complex sentences according to their logical relations:

1. To describe a reason and a consequence (because, because of)

Basic structure: 因为 + reason, 所以 + result
Optional: 因为 (因，由于)...所以 (而，从而，于是，因此，因而)...

Examples:

航班因天气原因而被推迟。
The flight is delayed due to bad weather.
Key words: 航班 airline　天气 weather　原因 reason, cause　推迟 to delay

他因病而没能参加演出。
He failed to take part in the show because he was sick.
Key words: 病 sick; sickness　参加 to join, to participate　演出 show

Chapter 8 Constructing Complex Sentences

因为我觉得不舒服，所以今天没上班。
I did not go to work because I felt sick.
Key words: 觉得 to feel 不 no, not 舒服 comfort 今天 today 没 no, not 上班 to go to work

他由于勤奋工作从而取得了很好的业绩。
Due to his diligence, he had great success in his work.
Key words: 他 he, him 工作 work 勤奋 diligent 取得 to gain 业绩 achievement, success

If there is an obvious and natural logical relation between two incidents, we can use part of the words, or even none of them. For example:

我觉得不舒服，所以今天没有上班。
我觉得不舒服，今天没有上班。
I did not go to work because I felt sick.

Note: This mechanism also works in some of the following cases.

之所以...是因为 (由于，因)...is typically used to emphasize a reason:

我之所以今天没有上班，是因为我觉得不舒服。
The reason I did not go to work is that I felt sick.
Key words: 今天 today 没 no, not 上班 to go to work 觉得 to feel 舒服 comfortable

他之所以在学习汉语方面进步很快，是由于他付出了很大的努力。
The reason he had such rapid progress learning Chinese is that he made a solid effort.
Key words: 学习 to learn 汉语 Chinese 方面 aspect 进步 to make progress 付出 to pay out 努力 effort

2. To describe an essential precondition for a consequence (only ...when..., only ...if)

Basic structure: 只有 + precondition, 才+ the consequence.
Optional: 只有 (仅有, 除非)...才 (方, 方可, 才可)...

Examples:

只有我们尊重别人，别人才会尊重我们。
Only when we respect others, will others respect us.
Key words: 我们 we, us 尊重 to respect 别人 other people

工厂仅有按时交货才可收到钱。
The factory receives payment only when it makes the delivery on time.
Key words: 工厂 factory 按时 on time 交货 to deliver the goods 收到 to receive 钱 money

Chapter 8 Constructing Complex Sentences

我们(只有)明天早上九点出发方能赶上飞机。
We can catch the flight only if we set off at 9 o'clock in the morning.
Key words: 明天 tomorrow 早上 morning   出发 to set off   赶 to catch 飞机 airplane

(只有) 使用合适的工具我们才能把汽车修好。
We can repair the car only if we have the right tools to do it.
Key words: 使用 to use   合适 proper   工具 tool 汽车 vehicle, car 修 to repair 好 good

3. To describe a consequent caused by a precondition (once…, as long as…)

Basic structure: 只要 + condition, 就 + consequence
Optional words: 只要（一旦, 一）… 就（便）…

Examples:

人一到齐我们就出发。
We will leave once everyone is here.
Key words: 到 to come 齐 all 出发 to leave, to set off

他一坐车就会感到恶心。
He feels nauseated when he travels by car.
Key words: 他 he, him 坐 to sit 车 vehicle 感到 to feel 恶心 sick, nauseated

一旦出现异常情况我们就停止行动。
We will call the mission off should anything unusual occur.
Key words: 出现 to appear 异常 abnormal 情况 situation 停止 to stop 行动 to move

只要我按下这个按钮，窗户就会被打开。
The window will open once I push this button down.
Key words: 我 I, me 按下 to push down 这个按钮 this button 窗户 window 打开 to open

4. To describe two actions (or incidents) happening in succession in a short time. (as soon as, soon after)

Basic structure: 一 + the previous action + 就 + the following action
Optional: 一 (刚, 刚刚, 才)…就…

Examples:

这本小说一上市就受到广泛欢迎。
This book was well received as soon as it appeared on the market.
Key words: 这本小说 this novel 上市 (be) on market 受到 to receive 广泛 popularly

他刚到电影院电影就开始了。
The movie began soon after he arrived.

Chapter 8 Constructing Complex Sentences

Key words: 到 to reach, to arrive 电影院 cinema 电影 movie 开始 to start, to begin

我们才休息了一会就开始爬山了。
After we took a short rest, we continued to climb the mountain.
Key words: 休息 rest 一会 a short time 开始 to start, to begin 爬山 to climb the mountain

夜幕刚刚降临大街上就没什么人了。
Soon after it turned dark, there were few people in the street.
Key words: 夜 night 幕 curtain 降临 to arrive, to fall 大街 street

5. To make a suppose (if...)

Basic structure: 如果 + an incident as a suppose + 就 + consequence
Optional: 如果 (要是，假如，假设，倘若，假使，若)...就 (便)...

Examples:

要是有人来找我，你便说我不在。
If anybody comes for me, say I am not in.
Key words: 来 to come 找 to find 说 to say

这个问题如果早点被发现，就不会有这个事故了。
This accident would never have happen if that problem had been discovered earlier.
Key words: 问题 question 早点 earlier 发现 to find 事故 accident

如果明天天气不好，我们就待在家里看电视。
If the weather is bad tomorrow, we will stay home and watch TV.
Key words: 明天 tomorrow 天气 weather 待 to stay 家里 at home 电视 television

假如他没打那个电话，他一定就会后悔。
He would have regretted it if he had not made that phone call.
Key words: 打那个电话 to make that phone call 一定 certainly 会 will 后悔 to regret

6. To make a deduction (since...then...)

Basic structure: 既然 + incident, 就 + deduction
Optional: 既然(既) + incident, 就(便) + deduction (since...then...)

Examples:

我们既然承诺帮助你，那么就一定会做到。
Since we promised to help you, then we certainly will do that.
Key words: 承诺 to promise 帮助 to help 一定 certainly, surely 做到 (to be) done

目前情况既已发生了变化，我们便需要调整计划。

160

Since things changed, we need to adjust our plan.
Key words: 情况 situation 发生 to happen 变化 change 调整 to modify 计划 plan

这件事(既然)和你无关，你(就)没必要管那么多。
Since this matter is none of your business, you need not be concerned about it.
Key words: 和 with 无关 to be unconcerned 必要 necessary 管 to manage

他既然认识到自己的错误了，我们就不要再责怪他。
Since he is aware of his mistake, we should stop blaming him.
Key words: 认识 to realize 错误 mistake 不要 not to 再 any more 责怪 to blame

7. To describe a transition in meanings (but, though, although).

Basic structure: 虽然 + incident as a condition, 但是 + incident as a transition
Optional: 虽然 (虽, 尽管)…但是 (但, 可是, 然而, 可是)

Examples:

虽然我觉得不舒服，但是我还坚持工作。
Although feeling sick, I still kept working.
Key words: 觉得 to feel 不舒服 uncomfortable 还 yet, still 坚持 to keep on 工作 work

Note: 还 or 仍 (仍然) indicates that something remains in a certain state.

他年纪虽小，可是胆识却很过人。
Although he is very young, he has remarkable courage and insight.
Key words: 年纪 age 小 small, little 胆识 courage and insight 过人 exceeding

尽管这个老人一个人生活，然而他并不觉得孤独。
Although this old man lived alone, he never felt lonely.
Key words: 这个老人 this old man 一个人 oneself 生活 live 并 yet 觉得 feel 孤独 lonely

这个工作虽困难，但不是没有可能解决。
Difficult as this work is, there must be a way to solve it.
Key words: 这个工作 this work 困难 difficult 可能 possibility 解决 to settle down

我虽然和他一同工作过一段时间，但却一点不了解他。
Although I worked with him for a while, I know nothing about him.
Key words: 一同 together 工作 to work 一段 a period of time 了解 to know, to understand

8. To describe a purpose (for, in order to).

Basic structure: 为了 + description of a purpose, + action for that purpose
Optional words: 为了 (为, 为着)…

Chapter 8 Constructing Complex Sentences

Examples:

为了尽快回家，他一路上开的都很快。
He drove very fast in order to get back home as soon as possible.
Key words: 尽快 as soon as possible 一路上 all the way 开 to drive 很快 very fast

我为了把汉语学好花了几年时间。
To learn Chinese well, I spent several years on it.
Key words: 汉语 the Chinese language 学好 to learn well 花 to spend 几年 several years

为买那套房子，这对夫妻攒了很长时间钱。
This couple has been saving money for a long time in order to buy that house.
Key words: 买 to buy 这对夫妻 this couple 攒 to collect 很长时间 a long time 钱 money

为了后代的幸福，我们应该减少消耗自然资源。
We should reduce our consumption of natural resources for the wellbeing of future generations.
Key words: 后代 offspring 幸福 happiness 减少 to reduce 消耗 to consume 自然 nature

The following structure is popularly used to emphasize purpose:

Action for a purpose+以+ the description of the purpose.

Note: In addition to 以, we also can use 以便，以求，用以，好，为的是 in this structure.

Examples:

我们应经常运动以提高身体素质。
We should exercise often to build up our health.
Key words: 经常 often 运动 to do physical exercise 提高 to enhance 素质 quality

你应该多找几个人谈谈你的想法以获得更多的建议。
You should find more people to discuss your idea with and get more advice.
Key words: 找 to find 谈谈 to talk 想法 idea 获得 to get 建议 advice, suggestion

他往前走了几步好看得更清楚一点。
He took a few steps forward to see more clearly.
Key words: 往前 forward 几步 several steps 看 to watch 更 more 清楚 clear 一点 a little

请把房间清理一下以便客人早点休息。
Please clean the room so that the guests can rest soon.
Key words: 请 please 房间 room 清理一下 to clean 客人 guest 早点 soon 休息 to rest

以免（免得，省得）is frequently used instead of 以 to express negative meanings. For example:

Chapter 8 Constructing Complex Sentences

政府开始控制汽车数量以免空气质量恶化。
The government started controlling the number of cars to avoid further deterioration of the air quality.
Key words: 政府 government 控制 to control 数量 quantity 质量 quality 恶化 to worsen

你做运动时应注意安全以免(免得, 省得)受伤。
When you do physical exercise, you should be careful not to injure yourself.
Key words: 做运动 to do physical exercise 注意 to care 安全 safe 受伤 (to be) injured

好 or 好让 is frequently used in spoken language to describe an expected result. Examples:

我们要快点走好赶上火车。
We had better walk faster to catch the train.
Key words: 快点 faster 走 to go, to walk 赶上 to catch 火车 train

这些日子他一直在安慰她，好让她尽快开始新的生活。
These days, he has been comforting her so she would start a new life as soon as possible.
Key words: 这些日子 these days 一直 always 安慰 to comfort, to console 尽快 as soon as possible 开始 to begin, to start 新的 new, fresh 生活 life; live

9. To extend a contrast (on the contrary, rather than)

Basic structure: 不但+ expected incident, 反而+ unexpected incident
Optional: 不但 (不仅, 非但)...反而 (反倒, 反过来)...

Examples:

最近物价不但没有降，反而快速上升。
Rather than fall, the prices have risen rapidly lately.
Key words: 最近 recently 物价 price 降 to fall 快速 rapidly 上升 to rise

我没想到你非但不感谢我，反倒生我的气。
I never realized you were angry instead of grateful.
Key words: 想到 to think of 感谢 to thank 生气 to be angry with

他不但没有觉得自己有错，反而认为别人做得不对。
He never thought things were his fault; on the contrary, he always believed that others were wrong.
Key words: 觉得 to feel 自己 oneself 错 mistake 别人 other people 不对 wrong

这辆车不但没有立即停下，反而掉头开走了。
Rather than stopping immediately, that car turned around and drove away.
Key word: 立即 at once 停下 to stop 掉头 to turn around 开走 to drive away

10. To describe two parallel states (both...and..., on one hand...on the other hand..., at the same time)

Basic structure: 既 + incident (state) + 又 + incident (state)
Optional: 又...又..., 又...也..., 一方面...另一方面..., 一方面...同时又...

Examples:

这件事情既复杂又敏感。
This matter is both complicated and sensitive.
Key words: 复杂 complicated 敏感 sensitive

目前我们既不能前进，也不能后退。
We can neither proceed nor retreat now.
Key words: 目前 at present time 不能 can not 前进 to proceed 后退 to draw back

他既具备实际工作能力，又能妥善处理人际关系。
He has the ability to handle both the practical parts of his job and his relationships with others.
Key words: 具备 to have 实际 practical 妥善 appropriately 人际关系 social relation

我一方面想很快见到她，同时又担心到时的尴尬。
On the one hand, I want to see her immediately; on the other hand, I am afraid the situation will be awkward.
Key words: 想 to want 很快 soon 见到 see 担心 afraid 到时 at the time 尴尬 awkward

11. To list possible choices (either...or...)

Basic structure: 或者 + choice, 或者 + choice
Optional: 要么...要么... 要不...要不...

Examples:

最后的赢家或者是你，或者是他。
The final winner will be either you or him.
Key words: 最后 final 赢家 winner

或者你来我家，或者我去你家。
Either you come to my home, or I go to yours.
Key words: 你 you 来 to come 我家 my home 去 to go 你家 your home

我们要么坐公共汽车，要么打车。
We can take either the bus or a taxi.
Key words: 我们 we, us 坐 to sit, to take 公共汽车 bus 打车 to take a taxi

这个工作你要不自己来做，要不交给别人去做。
You can either do this job yourself or hand it off to others.
Key words: 这个工作 this job 自己 oneself 来 to come 交给 to give to 别人 other people

12. To propose a better choice (had better… than)

Basic structure: 与其+ a possible choice, 不如+ better choice
Optional words: 与其 (若) + one choice, 不如 (不若) + better choice

Note: a popular of saying this in spoken language is: one choice, 还不胜 + better choice

Examples:

(与其) 临渊羡鱼，不如退而结网。
It is better to go back and make a net than to stand by the pond wishing for a fish.
Key words: 临 aside 渊 bank, shore 羡 to admire 鱼 fish 退 to withdraw 结网 to knit a net

他现在摸黑走，还不如天亮了再走。
It would be better for him to leave in the morning than go in the dark now.
Key words: 现在 now 摸黑 (to be) in dark 走 to walk 天亮 sunrise 再 then 走 to go

与其说他被对手打败了，还不如说是被他自己打败了。
It is better to say that he beat himself than to say that his opponents beat him.
Key words: 对手 opponent 打败 to defeat, to beat 自己 oneself

我们与其坐在房间里凭空猜测，不如去走出去调查这件事的真相。
It would be better to go find out the truth than sit at home wondering about it.
Key words: 凭空 by air 猜测 to suspect 走出去 to walk out 真相 truth

13. To describe a certainty in spite of a supposed condition (even that)

Basic structure: 即使+ a supposed condition +也+ incident as a certainty
Optional words: 即使 (纵然, 纵使, 就算, 就是, 即便, 哪怕)…也 (都, 仍, 还, 也都, 也还)…

Examples:

即使最聪明的人也不能解决这个问题。
Even the smartest man cannot solve this problem.
Key words: 聪明 smart 解决 to resolve 问题 problem

即使明天天气不好，我也会来看望你。
Even if the weather is bad, I will still come to see you tomorrow.
Key words: 天气 weather 也 still 会 will, can 来 to come 看望 to visit

他纵然承受了很大的压力也从不抱怨。
He never complained even though he was under a lot of pressure.
Key words: 承受 bear, carry on 很大 very large, a lot of 压力 pressure 抱怨 complain

我们即便面临严峻的挑战，仍不能放弃。
We should never give up even if we face a serious challenge.
Key words: 面临 to face 严峻 austere 挑战 challenge 放弃 to give up

In addition to the above, the followings structures are also popularly used:

Basic Structure: 无论+ a supposed condition +也+ incident as a certainty (no matter how, what, when, etc.)
Optional: 无论 (再, 不管, 任, 任凭, 哪怕)...也 (都, 也都)...

Examples:

再聪明的人都会犯错。
No matter how smart they are, anyone can make a mistake.
Key words: 聪明 wise, smart 人 people 犯错 to make a mistake

面对这么危险的任务，无论多谨慎也都不过分。
You cannot be too careful when faced with such a dangerous mission.
Key words: 面对 to face, to confront 危险 dangerous 谨慎 cautious 过分 excessive

无论这个工作多困难，我今天都得把它弄完。
I must finish this job today no matter how difficult it is.
Key words: 多 many, much 困难 difficulty 得 should 弄完 to finish

哪怕你和我的距离遥远，都挡不住我对你的思念。
No matter how far apart we are, nothing can stop me from missing you.
Key words: 距离 distance 遥远 far 挡住 to stop, to prevent 对 to, about 思念 to miss

14. To emphasize the subjective preference in choice (would rather...than...)

Basic structure: 宁可+ the incident as a cost +也+ the preferred choice
Optional: 宁可 (宁愿, 宁肯)...也 (都, 也都)...

Examples:

我们宁可通宵工作，也要完成这项实验。
We would rather work all night to finish this experiment.
Key words: 通宵 all night 工作 work, job 完成 to complete 这项实验 this experiment

中国的很多父母宁可花很多钱也要把自己的孩子送到一个好学校。
Many parents in China would rather spend a lot to send their children to good schools.
Key words: 父母 parents 花钱 to spend 孩子 kids 送 to send 学校 school

他宁愿自己省吃俭用，都要帮助那些贫穷的人。
He would rather pinch and scrape to help the poor.

Chapter 8 Constructing Complex Sentences

Key words: 省吃俭用 to pinch and scrape 帮助 to help 那些 those 贫穷 poor

目前很多年轻人宁肯花费很多时间和金钱创业也不愿当雇员。
Now, many young people would rather spend their time and money establishing their own business rather than work as employees of someone else.
Key words: 目前 at the present time 年轻人 youth, young people 花费 to spend 创业 to create one's own business 当 work as; be as 雇员 employee

Based on the above, we can integrate a series of sentences into a complex whole through intricate logical relations. For example:

虽然昨天他答应来准时来开会，但是到现在还没有来，所以他可能遇到麻烦了，因为他一直都很守时。
Although he promised to be at this meeting on time, he has not come. He must have some problem because he is always punctual.

因为我不同意他观点，所以我不会支持他，即使他试图强加于我，我也决不会改变我的立场。
 I will not support him because I do not agree with his opinion. I will not change my mind, even if he tries to force his ideas on me.

We can also use a complex sentence as an independent word, and integrate it into another sentence. Take the following sentence for example:

如果你工作努力，你就会被提升。
You will be promoted if you work hard.
Key words: 你 you 工作 to work 努力 hard 会 will, can 提升 to promote

This sentence can be integrated into other sentences:

我们相信如果你工作努力，你就会被提升。
We believe you will be promoted if you work hard.

如果你工作努力，你就会被提升是自然的事。
Of course, you will be promoted if you work hard.

Other examples:

他一遇到困难就退缩让我们很失望。
We are disappointed he always retreats when he runs into difficulty.
Key words: 一…就… once; as long as 遇到 to face 退缩 to retreat 失望 disappointed

我的建议是与其在这里等，不如立即采取行动。
My suggestion is we take immediate action rather than waiting.
Key words: 建议 suggestion 与其…不如… had better than 立即 at once 采取 to adopt

Chapter 8 Constructing Complex Sentences

教练告诉他的队员只要他们坚持下去，球队就能拿冠军。
The coach told his team that they could be the champions as long as they kept at it.
Key words: 教练 coach 告诉 to tell 队员 team member 只要...就... as long as 坚持下去 to keep on 球队 team 拿 to take, to get 冠军 champion

 Extra Knowledge: The Use of Punctuations in Chinese

The following is a list of the most commonly used punctuations in the Chinese language. Most of them have the same appearance and function as those used in English.

Punctuation	Brief introduction
。	Marks an end of a sentence.
，	Marks a break in a sentence, or separates a group of sentences.
？	Marks a question.
！	Marks an exclamation or strong mood.
、	Separates parallel ideas.
；	Separates parallel sentences.
：	What follows proves or explains what is referred to before.
——	Makes an explanation.
（ ）	Makes additional explanation.
……	Represents elided content.
《 》	Marks a name of articles, books, etc.
" "	Quotes somebody's words, or implies special meaning.
~	Connects relative meanings.
.	Emphasizes words.

Chapter 9
Advanced Skills in Making Sentences

Let us begin with a brief review of the contents of the previous chapters.

In the first two chapters, we discussed the basic features of Chinese characters and the special and unique mechanisms for combining independent characters to create new words. A single character usually contains a group of meanings that originated from one or two core meanings. A precondition for any combination is that there should be a logical relation in the meanings.

In Chapter 3, we introduced 22 basic rules for creating new words. These rules correspond to the universal logical models, which not only exist in the Chinese language but also in other languages. These models make it possible to create numerous words with only a small quantity of characters.

In Chapter 4, we extended the basic rules into universal cases. By repeatedly applying the rules for combining words, we can create complicated combinations (most are complex words) with ever more intricate meanings. We also discussed some basic skills in creating complex words.

In Chapter 5, we discussed the essence of sentences, and introduced several typical structures corresponding to various functions of communication. Some of these are extensions of the basic rules for combining words. Although there was nothing new, we covered skills on organizing individual bits of meanings into a whole.

In Chapter 6, we introduced the use of various tenses. By adding words functioning as tense indicators, and the mutual cultural background, we created sentences that referred to past, present and future conditions.

In Chapter 7, we introduced the formulation of various kinds of questions. There are two important methods of forming a question: One is to add a specific word (like 吗, 是否, 是不是) into a sentence asking for confirmation, the other is to substitute the unknown component with a specific word.

In Chapter 8, we introduced the basic mechanism for integrating two (or more) sentences into a complex sentence and covered the most common cases of this process.

Chapter 9 Advanced Skills in Making Sentences

As we have noted repeatedly, practical language use decides the grammar, not the reverse. So, some skills and structures, especially those in the later chapters, can only be regarded as models for quick reference and quick application.

In some cases, the arrangement of words in a sentence can be very flexible. Omitting words also frequently happens. There are some principles and skills in doing so, but we should first delve deeper into the core of this ancient language with the help of an interesting illustration.

There are 20 characters surrounding the circle above. They are:

舟 boat
沙 sand
晴 clear sky; shining
椰 coconut palm
艳 gorgeous, color
淡 flat, weak; to weaken
渡 ferry

绕 to circle, to coil
白 white; to whiten
芳 balmy, fragrant
幽 deep and remote
华 flashy, prosperous
星 star
斜 to incline; inclined

乱 random; to disarray
岸 bank, shore
树 tree
岛 island
月 moon
荒 deserted

We can start from any character in the circle, and then divide them clockwise into four sections of five characters. No matter where we start, we get a complete and meaningful Chinese poem. For example:

Start from 舟	Start from 乱	Start from 沙	Start from 白
舟绕乱沙白	乱沙白岸晴	沙白岸晴芳	白岸晴芳树
岸晴芳树椰	芳树椰幽岛	树椰幽岛艳	椰幽岛艳华
幽岛艳华月	艳华月淡星	华月淡星荒	月淡星荒渡
淡星荒渡斜	荒渡斜舟绕	渡斜舟绕乱	斜舟绕乱沙

Chapter 9 Advanced Skills in Making Sentences

We can create 20 different poems in this manner, which is not possible in any other language in the world. Two unique features of the Chinese language make this possible:

1. A character usually contains a group of diverse meanings originated from one or two core meanings. This allows a character to interact with others flexibly and reasonably.

2. People's universal cognitive background and experience play an important role when they try to organize the pieces of meanings into a reasonable and complete concept. It is something like guessing the meaning of a riddle: People are given a very limited number of hints and must find the answer by aide of their personal knowledge and experience. That is why Chinese can sometimes omit inessential words in a sentence.

The above case is an extreme situation, however. In the next case, we will not discuss the complex linguistic philosophy beneath the surface, but introduce some practical skills to make use of the principles and rules flexibly and freely.

Here is a sentence one hears frequently:

您吃晚饭了吗？
Have you had supper?

In spoken language, all the following formulations are acceptable:

您晚饭吃了吗？
晚饭您吃了吗？
晚饭吃了吗您？
吃晚饭了吗您？

Because people can easily deduce the meaning from the words they hear, we can arrange the words with flexible sequences. Another example:

昨天我在公司遇到他了。
我昨天在公司遇到他了。
昨天在公司我遇到他了。
I met him at the company yesterday.

All the above sentences are acceptable, but in theory, we can also say:

我在公司昨天遇到他了。
在公司我昨天遇到他了。
昨天在公司遇到他了我。

Chapter 9 Advanced Skills in Making Sentences

However, these formulations do not fit the customary use of the language. The following examples show how to omit the nonessential words in a reasonable way.

杯子被打碎了。
A glass is broken.
Key words: 杯子 glass 打碎 to break

This sentence is structured in EP-1, and 被 is specifically used to indicate a passive voice. It is common sense that a glass cannot break itself, so someone must have done it. Thus, we can omit 被 in this sentence:

杯子打碎了。
A glass is broken.

Another example:

汽车加油了吗？
Has the car been fueled?
Key words: 汽车 car, vehicle 加油 to fuel

所有的工作都干完了。
All of the work has been finished.
Key words: 所有 all 工作 work 都 all, totally 干完 to finish

他说的话都记下来了。
Everything he said was recorded.
Key words: 他说的话 the words he said 都 all, totally 记下来 to record

This mechanism can also be extended to universal cases. For example:

把门关上！
门关上！
Close the door!
Key words: 门 door 关上 to shut, to close

两本书的价格一共是25元。
两本书一共25元。
The price of the two books is 25 yuan.
Key words: 两本书 two books 价格 price 一共 total; totally 元 yuan

你要是看到他就告诉我。
你看到他就告诉我。
Tell me if you see him.
Key words: 要是…就… if…then 看到 to see, to find 告诉 to tell

Chapter 9 Advanced Skills in Making Sentences

如果你有困难就来找我。
有困难就找我。
You can come for me if you have any trouble.
Key words: 如果…就…if…then… 有 to have 困难 difficulty, trouble 找 to seek, to search

因为我没见到他，所以我就提前回家了。
我没见到他就提前回家了。
Because I did not find him, I came back home early.
Key words: 因为…所以… because; 见到 to see, to find 提前 in advance 回家 to go home

Omitting inessential words is very popular in daily dialogue. For example:

如果明天下雨，你就别来了，如果真有什么事，我们就在电话里说。
明天下雨你就别来了，真有什么事就在电话里说。
If it rains tomorrow, you need not come here. If there is anything urgent, we can talk on the phone.

如果明天来的客人多，你就多派几个人在门口维持秩序。
明天客人多，你就多派几个人在门口维持秩序。
If too many guests come, you should assign more people at the gate to maintain order.

这些桌子要被摆成三排，椅子也要被摆好，另外你要找人测试一下音响设备。
这些桌子摆三排，椅子也摆好，另外找人测试一下音响。
These tables should be put in three rows, and the chairs should be put in position. What's more, you should find someone to test the audio equipment.

Chapter 9 Advanced Skills in Making Sentences

 Extra Knowledge: Art of Wording and Phrasing

Based on powerful characters and a flexible grammar system, it is easy to develop various language styles both in content and in form. That is to say, the unique properties of the Chinese language give people considerable freedom in wording and phrasing.

In Chinese history, many types of literature with specific styles and forms have appeared. The following are samples of the master works of various historical periods. Although they differ from the language as it is now used, they express highly developed skills in wording and phrasing.

---

a poem written about 3,000 years ago:

关关雎鸠，在河之洲。

窈窕淑女，君子好逑。

参差荇菜，左右流之。

窈窕淑女，寤寐求之。

《关雎》

---

an article written about 2,500 years ago:

十年春，齐师伐我。公将战。曹刿请见。其乡人曰："肉食者谋之，又何间焉？"刿曰："肉食者鄙，未能远谋。"乃入见。问："何以战？"公曰："衣食所安，弗敢专也，必以分人。"……

《曹刿论战》，《左传》

---

an article written about 2,000 years ago:

……孔子曰："求！君子疾夫舍曰'欲之'而必为之辞。丘也闻有国有家者，不患寡而患不均，不患贫而患不安。盖均无贫，和无寡，安无倾。夫如是，故远人不服，则修文德以来之；既来之，则安之……"。……

《季氏将伐颛臾》，《论语》

---

the lyrics of a folk song about 2,000 years ago:

上邪！我欲与君相知，长命无绝衰。山无陵，江水为竭，冬雷阵阵，夏雨雪，天地合，乃敢与君绝！

《上邪》，《汉铙歌十八曲》

---

an article written about 1,300 years ago:

……闾阎扑地，钟鸣鼎食之家；舸舰弥津，青雀黄龙之轴。虹销雨霁，彩彻区明。落霞与孤鹜齐飞，秋水共长天一色……

王勃，《滕王阁序》

Chapter 9 Advanced Skills in Making Sentences

a poem written about 1,300 years ago:

朝辞白帝彩云间

千里江陵一日还

两岸猿声啼不住

轻舟已过万重山

李白，《早发白帝城》

a poetry written about 900 years ago:

莫听穿林打叶声，何妨吟啸且徐行。

竹杖芒鞋轻胜马，谁怕，一蓑烟雨任平生。

料峭春风吹酒醒，微冷，山头斜照却相迎。

回首向来萧瑟处，归去，也无风雨也无晴。

苏轼，《定风波》

a script for a drama written about 450 years ago:

旦：梦回莺啭，乱煞年光遍。人立小庭深院。

贴：炷尽沉烟，抛残绣线，恁今春关情似去年？

旦：晓来望断梅关，宿妆残。

贴：你侧着宜春髻子恰凭阑。

旦：剪不断，理还乱，闷无端。

贴：已分付催花莺燕借春看。

旦：春香，可曾叫人扫除花径？

贴：分付了。

旦：取镜台衣服来。

〔贴取镜台衣服上〕

……

汤显祖，《牡丹亭》

a novel written about 300 years ago:

……宝玉早已看见多了一个姊妹，便料定是林姑妈之女，忙来作揖。厮见毕归坐，细看形容，与众各别：两弯似蹙非蹙笼烟眉，一双似喜非喜含情目。态生两靥之愁，娇袭一身之病。泪光点点，娇喘微微。闲静时如姣花照水，行动处如弱柳扶风。心较比干多一窍，病如西子胜三分。……

曹雪芹，《红楼梦》

Chapter 9　Advanced Skills in Making Sentences

> a novel written about 80 years ago:
>
> ……
>
> 　　阿Q没有家，住在未庄的土谷祠里；也没有固定的职业，只给人家做短工，割麦便割麦，春米便春米，撑船便撑船。工作略长久时，他也或住在临时主人的家里，但一完就走了。所以，人们忙碌的时候，也还记起阿Q来，然而记起的是做工，并不是"行状"；一闲空，连阿Q都早忘却，更不必说"行状"了。只是有一回，有一个老头子颂扬说："阿Q真能做！"这时阿Q赤着膊，懒洋洋的瘦伶仃的正在他面前，别人也摸不着这话是真心还是讥笑，然而阿Q很喜欢。
>
> ……
>
> 　　　　　　　　　　　　　　——鲁迅，《阿Q正传》

后 记

　　《汉语语法新通路》的修订版和大家见面了，修订版在延续第一版的理论基础和内容框架的基础上，大量增加了新的内容，包括理论本身的改进、增加诸多实用的功能、增加大量范例等等，内容扩充了近一倍。无论如何，这本书的目标没有变化，还是想让海外的汉语学习者能够"一看就懂，一学就用"，真正发挥语法应有的功能，让学习汉语更富效率。

　　"大道至简"。正是因为汉语的简单，使她得以传袭数千年，始终成为聚拢中华大家庭最为重要的纽带。"简"的外在表现是汉语极具特色的语法规则，"简"的核心在于极其人性化的语言思维与组织方式，而这种独特的思维方式背后则是中华民族精妙的哲学。

　　"道生一，一生二，二生三，三生无数"这句话，应当是对汉语语法内在特质最为精当的概括。本书力求简单实用，向海外学习者展现汉语智慧与美，彰显运用之便利，以帮助海内外学习者轻松高效掌握汉语基础应用。

　　在此书编写过程中，得到来自家人、师长、朋友的无私支持和帮助，也得到华语教学出版社的大力支持，在此表示由衷的感谢！本人深感能在盛世之时，尽砖瓦之力，传播汉语，昌扬中华语言与文化，实为人生幸事。

作　者

作者介绍
About the Author

周晓更
生于 1975 年 3 月
硕士学位
获国家《汉语作为外语教学能力证书（高级）》
编写《汉语世界》教材 "十五"国家重点音像出版规划项目）
编写《汉语作为外语教学能力考试应试技巧（中、高级）》

Zhou Xiaogeng
Born in March 1975
Master of Arts
Acquirement of **Qualification Certificate of Teaching Chinese as a Foreign Language (Advanced)**
Author of textbook of **Chinese World** (a state sponsored project of multimedia learning materials publication)
Author of **Directory on Acquiring Qualification Certificate of Teaching Chinese as a Foreign Language**

作者邮箱 Author's E-mail:　zhouxiaogeng@163.com

责任编辑：郭　辉
封面设计：王　薇
印刷监制：佟汉东

图书在版编目（CIP）数据

汉语语法新通路 / 周晓更编著. —修订本. —北京：华语教学出版社，2009
ISBN 978-7-80200-613-3

Ⅰ. 汉… Ⅱ. 周… Ⅲ. 汉语－语法－对外汉语教学－教学参考资料　Ⅳ. H195.4

中国版本图书馆 CIP 数据核字（2009）第 107492 号

汉语语法新通路 修订版
周晓更　编著

*

©华语教学出版社
华语教学出版社出版
（中国北京百万庄大街 24 号　邮政编码 100037）
电话：(86)10-68320585
传真：(86)10-68326333
网址：www.sinolingua.com.cn
电子信箱：hyjx@sinolingua.com.cn
北京外文印刷厂印刷
中国国际图书贸易总公司海外发行
（中国北京车公庄西路 35 号）
北京邮政信箱第 399 号　邮政编码 100044
新华书店国内发行
2009 年（大 16 开）第一版
（汉英）
ISBN 978-7-80200-613-3

定价：29.00 元